BUSH PILOTS OF ALASKA

BUSH PILOTS
OF ALASKA

Photographs by Fred Hirschmann

Text by Kim Heacox

Preface by Lowell Thomas, Jr.

Afterword by Jay Hammond

GRAPHIC ARTS CENTER PUBLISHING®

To Bernd Gaedeke, Glenn Hittson, Mike Ivers, Mike Reynolds, Barbara Shallcross, and Frank Taylor—and all the other pilots who have given their lives while flying in Alaska.

FRED HIRSCHMANN

TABLE OF CONTENTS

Preface • Fun, Adventure, & Challenge   7
    Lowell Thomas, Jr.

Chapter One • Bit by the Bug   17
    Kim Heacox

Chapter Two • Anywhere You'll Ride, I'll Fly   33
    Kim Heacox

Chapter Three • The Denali Flyers   49
    Kim Heacox

Chapter Four • Don't Go Through the Looking Glass   81
    Kim Heacox

Chapter Five • The Haines Big Mac Attack   101
    Kim Heacox

Afterword • Reflections   129
    Jay Hammond

Acknowledgments   142
    Fred Hirschmann and Kim Heacox

International Standard Book Number 1-55868-012-8
Library of Congress Catalog Number 89-83730
©MCMLXXXIX by Graphic Arts Center Publishing Company
P.O. Box 10306 • Portland, Oregon 97296-0306 • 503/226-2402
Editor-in-Chief • Douglas A. Pfeiffer
Associate Editor • Jean Andrews
Designer • Robert Reynolds
Endsheet Illustrator • David Chandler
Book Manufacturing • Lincoln & Allen Co.
Printed in the United States of America
Sixth Printing

These photographs were taken with Mamiya 645 cameras utilizing 45mm, 80mm, 110mm, and 210mm lenses. A Ken-Lab Gyrostabilizer mounted below the medium-format camera damped aircraft vibration and turbulance.

■ *Half Title Page:* A formation of Super Cubs on skis over Knik Arm with the Talkeetna Mountains beyond. ■ *Frontispiece:* The Juneau Icefield and a Wings of Alaska Cessna 206. ■ *Title Page:* A Bush Pilots Air Service de Havilland DHC-2 Beaver above boreal forest and muskeg. ■ *Above:* John Hajdukovich, owner of Frontier Flying Service, in his Grumman Widgeon over the Brooks Range. ■ *Right:* Glenn Hittson and his Piper PA-18 Super Cub on an Arctic Ocean beach.

Preface

FUN, ADVENTURE, & CHALLENGE

by Lowell Thomas, Jr.

Lowell Thomas, Jr., a veteran glacier pilot, helps unload a climber's gear.

The sky was dark blue; the wind, light from the northeast; the air, minus 25 degrees Fahrenheit. The red-winged Helio Courier cruised over treeless snow-covered foothills of the Alaska Range. Veteran climbing guide Vern Tejas and I were at nine thousand feet, aiming for One Shot Pass and Denali's Kahiltna Glacier.

Behind our seats were enough food, fuel, and equipment to sustain Vern for a month—including an aluminum extension ladder, one end of which just missed the instrument panel while the other was up against the aft bulkhead. Later, that ladder would be invaluable as he traversed the lower Kahiltna with its snow-covered crevasses.

We flew through One Shot, over an icefall, and up the glacier, then turned into the shadows of the Southeast Fork. That is where Tejas, in 1988, began the first winter round-trip solo of Denali. He made it both ways, but we could not know that until I picked him up twenty-eight days later.

This book portrays the many facets of bush flying in Alaska and its continuing importance in a state twice the size of Texas but with only a few thousand miles of highway and just one railroad. Without aviation, particularly light single-engine airplanes, hundreds of villages would be totally isolated—no mail, no groceries, no way to get to the "big city," little access to fishing or hunting.

Flying the bush today is far safer and less work than fifty years ago. Aircraft then had less reliable engines, poor radios or none at all, few if any navigational aids, unheated cockpits year-round, and few available landing sites. What a challenge for pioneer pilots! Now engines are good for up to two thousand hours before overhaul; fuels are better; airports and strips are profuse; radios and nav-aids are excellent; blind flying instruments, hourly weather reports, and FAA traffic controllers using radar are the norm. All planes now have emergency locator beacons to aid in search and rescue. And we even have satellites to listen for ELT signals! What progress in less than a lifetime!

Left: Talkeetna Air Taxi's Helio Courier H-295 flies past 17,400-foot Mount Foraker en route to the Southeast Fork of Kahiltna Glacier.

However, much remains unchanged. Map reading and skilled piloting are still just as essential, especially in mountainous areas where the ability to read signs of wind, downdrafts, and turbulence is vital. In fact, the main obstacle today to a successful flight is the pilot—either a lack of skill and experience, or an attitude of overconfidence. As a longtime Alaskan pilot has said: "the cockpit is no place for an optimist." Another key to survival is an ability to say "NO!" Sounds simple enough, but . . .

In some three thousand hours of mountain and glacier flying in the past ten years in my wheel-ski Helio Courier, I have pushed hard against that margin of safety a time or two. Most often it has been a matter of weather and poor visibility, such as landing in whiteout conditions in support of climbers. However, my most harrowing moments have come from mechanical failure. Several summers ago, with no warning, my engine began to run extremely rough and the oil pressure gauge started sliding toward zero. Without oil, the engine would quickly grind to a screeching halt. Luckily, in the previous five minutes, I had climbed to four thousand feet. If I cut mixture and turned off the ignition, the propeller would continue to windmill, turning the engine until it seized. I pulled the plane up, bleeding off airspeed almost to a stall, put the prop in coarse pitch, mixture back, switch off. The prop stopped. I started losing altitude, holding airspeed at about fifty.

Through a hole, I spotted a few possible landing sites—sandbars in the Susitna River, a section of the Parks Highway that might work if nothing got in the way. Then a small gravel airstrip popped into view, and plane and I glided down to a happy deadstick landing. Later, my mechanic, Roger Borer, found the trouble: a broken oil scavenge pump in the turbo section. What if it had failed the day before, during the rescue of two frostbitten German climbers on Denali? To reach them at the 14,200-foot level, I had flown in and out over a thick cloud layer that obscured jagged peaks and broken glaciers below. Not a happy thought!

Another time lady luck was with me was shortly after takeoff from the gravel strip at Kantishna. I was homeward

Frost clings to a 1929 Curtiss Robin at Alaska Aviation Heritage Museum.

bound to Anchorage with two passengers after a day of flying visitors around the mountain. Suddenly a terrible vibration seized the plane. The engine cowling shook so violently I feared the engine would tear loose. Despite the violent shaking, the engine continued to run. Could we make it back to the airstrip? We did – to discover that four inches of one of the three propeller blades had torn off and disappeared. Why? Nobody knows. What if twelve inches of blade had broken off? The engine might have torn loose with unthinkable consequences.

Did I say "lady luck"? I am convinced that the good Lord has been my copilot many times. To keep things in perspective, in all my flying, including with the Air Force during World War II, I have experienced only five mechanical failures; all have ended happily with nary a crash.

A question often asked those who have moved to our 49th state is "how come?" Part of my answer has always been – aviation. Flying has always meant a lot to me, perhaps partly because my father was historian of man's first flight around the world back in 1924 – and because such famous aviators as Jimmy Doolittle, Eddie Rickenbacker and Frank Hawks were frequent visitors to our upstate New York home. I always wanted to fly, and realized my dream when I won my wings in what was then the Army Air Corps. Some years later, after marrying the daughter of a flying family – Tay's father was a vice president of Pan American Airways – my first plane was a sturdy little Stinson.

Then, in the summer of 1958, following years of work in New York City, I was asked to lead a film crew around Alaska for a TV "special" for my father's High Adventure series. Our purpose was to show the opportunities in our new state for young folks as well as to show its beauty. So Tay and I with our daughter, Anne, headed northwest in our love affair with Alaska, bringing us north as new residents.

Flying the Last Frontier can be a soul-stirring experience. One wings over endless miles of spruce forest sprinkled with shining lakes and ponds, with no sign of human habitation – only an occasional moose, or a bear with cubs, or perhaps a cluster of caribou. My own favorite area is

McKinley – "Denali" – with nearby Foraker and Hunter, all taller than any mountains in the Lower 48. Words alone cannot convey the awesome grandeur of these snow-girded giants. The pictures will do that far better.

I remember one lady who convinced me to put a public address system in my plane. I had turned in my seat occasionally to describe points of interest to my passengers. As I turned yet again to make a comment, this lady shouted: "Never mind, young man! Turn around and watch where we're going!" Anyway, a PA system was overdue.

Most enjoyable to me is transporting climbers who come from around the world. The 1988 season saw a record 887 on Denali alone, with several hundred more on nearby mountains. The average Denali success rate is about 60 percent. A few generally perish in the attempt, victims of crevasse falls, avalanches, pulmonary and cerebral edema, or occasionally just sheer exhaustion. And always there are cases of severe frostbite, for Denali can be brutally cold, down to minus 40 degrees Fahrenheit even in mid-summer.

Perhaps the most interesting climbers I have flown were ten Soviets in 1986. These were some of the strongest climbers in the USSR. Several had been to the top of Mount Everest and all had spent years climbing in the towering Pamirs. Once on the Kahiltna, they virtually ran up the mountain's west rib – up and down in seven days – quite a contrast to the usual two or three weeks.

Along with the fun and adventure, surely it is the many challenges of flying the Alaskan bush that keep luring us on. It is a challenge to reach one of our high-altitude landing sites, make a smooth upslope glacier landing, then fly out with a load of climbers and their gear, too often just as the weather begins to come down. And it is a challenge to know when to say "NO!" We"re going to wait for better weather!" Fun, adventure, and a challenge – those three words sum up for me what it means to fly Alaska's bush.

Right: Float planes link the villages of Southeast Alaska. A parade of Beavers lands and takes off from the Tongass Narrows by Ketchikan.

■ *Left:* A Certified Public Accountant, Rick Schikora flies his Cessna 170 above the Koyukuk River's North Fork to visit a client in Bettles. ■ *Above:* Nunataks and expanse of ice provide an inhospitable backdrop for a Wings of Alaska Cessna 206 on amphibious floats flying over the Juneau Icefield. ■ *Overleaf:* A gibbous moon rises over the Chugach Range beyond de Havilland Beavers and an Otter stored for winter at Bush Pilots Air Service along Lake Hood in Anchorage.

■ *Above:* An Alaskan workhorse, an Otter on floats is capable of hauling over two thousand pounds. Here, hunters of caribou and moose load their gear into an Otter at Pear Lake in Lake Clark National Preserve. ■ *Right:* Above the junction of the John and Koyukuk rivers, the midnight sun's pink glow catches the Bettles Lodge Cessna 185 ferrying hikers from Gates of the Arctic National Park. This Cessna 185 on floats has a useful payload of about eleven hundred pounds.

Chapter One

BIT BY THE BUG

by Kim Heacox

A license plate in Petersburg expresses a sentiment that is both clearly felt and heard in all parts of the state.

My nephew, Rob, came to Alaska in his nineteenth summer, one year out of high school, one year into college, a bit of a lost soul. School did not suit him; textbooks gave him a rash. A professional career seemed about as tangible as subatomic physics and existentialism. But the clock was ticking, and unbeknownst to Rob he stood at a point where we all stand at one time or another, a point where the simplest decisions have profound consequences and you embark on a path you follow the rest of your life. Rob's summer was beginning to shape up like all the rest—hanging out with friends in Spokane, Washington, watching girls, drinking beer—when he received a phone call from Glacier Bay Lodge. Would he like to spend the summer working in Alaska?

Two weeks later Rob stood on the dock at Bartlett Cove in Glacier Bay National Park, as a Cessna 206 on floats flew overhead. Planes of all types always had intrigued him, but this one was different. Backdropped by the shining Fairweather Range, the Cessna banked smoothly, purred over the spruce trees of Lester Island, and landed like poetry on the glass-still water. Twenty yards away the pilot cut the engine, worked the water rudders, and glided up to the dock. Rob dropped what he was doing and walked over.

The days wore into weeks, the weeks into months, and every time a float plane flew into Bartlett Cove, Rob was there, smiling. He had, as they say in the parlance of bush flying, been "bit by the bug." Suddenly, his life had gained direction; he wanted to be a pilot. Not just any pilot, but a bush pilot in Alaska.

If you mention bush pilots up here, some old-timers scowl and say, "There ain't no more bush pilots in Alaska. Nope, bush pilots flew when there weren't no airstrips or nav-aids (navigational aids) or FAA regulations all over the place. They used their wits and flew country that had never been flown before. They landed where they had to—on glaciers, river bars, tundra, lakes, the ocean. You name it.

Left: Pilot Ted Branstetter hauls diesel fuel in an Otter from Wrangell in Alaska to the Johnny Mountain Gold Mine in British Columbia.

And they flew planes before World War II when engines weren't nearly so reliable."

Perhaps the freedoms are not as high as they once were, but neither are the accident rates. And many contemporary private and commercial pilots insist that in logging thousands of hours over Alaska—a land still wild, big, beautiful, and unforgiving—they in fact become bush pilots. It is not like it used to be, but it is not like flying over California or Connecticut, either. The edge is sharper, the challenge greater, the adventure more acute. You still use your wits and learn both your own limits and those of your plane. You taxi into the wind, lift into the air, and watch Alaska—the Great Land—dropping below.

"The man who has dropped to a rough landing somewhere in the wilderness and seen people crowd around his plane for mail and meat will not again be content to slide monotonously along the concrete city airports of the main line," wrote Jean Potter in *The Flying North*. But her words apply today as well: "The man who has flown for hours alone above the northland, and mastered the techniques of doing so, will not again be content to be chained in traffic above a maze of roads, telephone poles, cities and towns." It is not just the thrill of flying, but the beauty of Alaska as well. Combined, they are as irresistible today as they were fifty years ago.

So Rob went back to Washington and spent three years earning his private and commercial licenses, along with his bachelor's degree in aeronautics. School suddenly began to appeal to him. He tended bar at night but seldom drank, choosing instead to fly the next morning. On the final written and practical exams, he scored at the top of his class. Everything looked good; soon he would carve his future in the skies of Alaska.

Then a major airlines representative came to the campus looking for candidates. Be a copilot in six years? A captain in twelve? Think of the prestige, travel, and good income. Rob vacillated.

But selfish uncle that I am, I wanted Rob to return to Alaska so we could fly together. So I told him a story about a

A Grumman G-21 Goose owned by the state trundles across a highway at Anchorage International Airport.

retired airlines captain who had visited Alaska to float down the Sheenjek River in the Arctic National Wildlife Refuge. A Cessna 185 carried him and his friends north out of Fort Yukon, over the Yukon Flats and a sea of muskeg and spruce, and toward the south side of the Brooks Range. Upon reaching the Sheenjek, the pilot flew low over the river and studied a wind sock in an alder next to a short gravel bar. He made another flyover and said, "She looks good." Everyone held on for a white-knuckle landing. The Cessna skimmed a bluff, kissed the gravel bar, rumbled towards the river and swung around with five feet to spare. The retired captain was flabbergasted. That afternoon he sat atop a hill and quietly watched the bush pilot bring the 185 in and out, ferrying gear, landing and taking off repeatedly without a hitch. As he watched the final flawless landing and takeoff he said, "You know, for thirty years all I really did was sit in the cockpit of a Boeing jet and run a computer. But this guy, he's a real pilot."

Granted, that is not a fair assessment of the work of commercial jet pilots—all of whom are highly trained and skilled professionals—nor is it a fair story to tell one's impressionable nephew who is trying to make career decisions. We talked it over, though, and as a footnote agreed that the seat-of-the-pants notoriety accorded Alaskan bush pilots is more a thing of the past than the present. Yet the past dies hard in the Last Frontier. Images linger. The names Eielson, Wien, Reeve, Crosson, Jefford, Ferguson, Barr, and Sheldon remain bigger than life. Good pilots in Alaska today realize they cannot achieve what those men did, because the times have changed and the rules are different. Many pilots could care less about notoriety. The myth that flying has to be dangerous to be adventurous is just that— a myth.

Though the bush pilot had landed along the Sheenjek River many times, he had also elected to pass it by when conditions were unsafe. The idea is to stay alive, stay in business. For all its immensity, Alaska is small. Only half a million people live here. The entire state is like a gossip-filled town where reputations cement quickly. If an air taxi

makes mistakes, frightens passengers, suffers accidents, or incurs penalties, soon everybody knows. From Kaktovik to Kotzebue, from Kenai to Ketchikan, it is survival of the safest. The business is only as risky as a pilot makes it. As the saying goes: "There are old pilots and bold pilots, but no old, bold pilots."

A good example is Harold Gillam, the boldest pilot of them all. "He thrill-em, chill-em, spill-em, but no kill-em Gillam," a third-grade Alaskan Native wrote about this quiet bulldog of a man with an inscrutable smile, bushy eyebrows, and the uncanny ability to fly almost anywhere at anytime. He crashed six times in his first six months, but that never stopped him. If anything, it gave him greater resolve, and he began to fly like a wizard. While half a dozen dispirited pilots would sit in a roadhouse playing poker and waiting for the weather to clear, Gillam would fly in, fuel up, and take off. Old-timers back then referred to three types of weather: "Pan-American weather," clear and calm; "ordinary weather," which most pilots would fly; and "Gillam weather." Some passengers said he was crazy and refused to fly with him; others said he was the best and they flew with no one else.

Throughout the 1930s, the mail service along the lower Kuskokwim River was sporadic at best. Villagers had no idea when the plane would arrive. But in 1938, Harold Gillam began flying the route and soon everyone could set their watches—not just to the day and hour, but to the minute—by the sound of his silver Pilgrim roaring through the clouds. Day after day, month after month, Gillam delivered the mail to twenty villages along the 525-mile route between Fairbanks and Bethel, never missing a stop, never arriving late.

But more than what he did, it was the way he did it— quietly, confidently, and with patented aplomb. In the middle of a snowstorm, he would casually walk out, check his plane, get in, and take off. It seemed no man could fly so boldly so long without the odds beating him, which they did in January 1943. Recently hired as chief pilot with Morrison-Knudson, Gillam was flying five passengers in a

Departing Seward, one of ERA's Bell 206-B Jet Rangers climbs above diesel engines of the Alaska Railroad.

twin-engine Lockheed Electra north from Seattle when he hit a bad storm and dense fog. Confused by a map that did not show the latest installation of navigational aids along the Ketchikan Range Leg, he circled Annette Island and tried to orient himself. But ice formed on the wings, an engine went out, and a downdraft plummeted the plane four thousand feet. Gillam got on the radio, "I'm in trouble. . . ." He gained control and barely missed one mountain, but not another, as the plane plowed into a forested slope. While Gillam and all the passengers survived the initial crash, in the end Gillam and a young woman died. The other passengers were rescued a month after the crash.

Alaska was stunned. Had Gillam run out of luck? Had his abilities diminished? Had he been living on tremendous skill all those years, or on borrowed time? The questions, like the legacy, will not go away.

Although many of the early bush pilots died in their planes; many more did not, and certainly, they accomplished great things. Perhaps one of the best examples is Noel Wien, one of the "old originals" in Alaskan aviation. He made the first flight between Anchorage and Fairbanks, the first aircraft landing north of the Arctic Circle, and the first transcontinental flight between Alaska and the Soviet Union. He brought three remarkable brothers to Alaska— Ralph, Fritz, and Sig. "Alaska," he once said, "keeps a fellow guessing. . . . It tugs at you all the time." He founded a successful airline company, received numerous awards, and died of old age.

My nephew nods when I tell him this, but his face betrays some skepticism. Maybe the money worries him. You do not get rich flying planes in Alaska. Lowell Thomas, Jr., the glacier pilot in Talkeetna, once told me, "If you want to make a small fortune in the air taxi business, you better start out with a large fortune. "No, Rob assures me, it is not the money that bothers him. He has the rest of his life to make money. Alaska "tugs at him all the time," but he has heard disturbing stories about pilots who graduated from his school years earlier and came to Alaska and died flying. It is the safety record, not the pay, that concerns him.

Though Alaska's air accident rate over the years has dropped significantly, it still averages higher than in the Lower 48 (seven percent higher in 1988). Between October 1987 and September 1988, Rob's last year in flight school, Alaska air taxi accidents and fatalities reached their highest level in ten years: thirty-eight accidents, seven of which caused thirty-four fatalities. Eighteen of those fatalities occurred when a Ryan Air Twin Beech crashed in Homer. A year-long investigation determined the cause was that the plane was improperly loaded. The Anchorage Division of the National Transportation Safety Board attributed the bad year to an influx of younger, less experienced pilots who were not familiar with risk management.

The media covers accidents thoroughly, but not the millions of hours of competent, uneventful flying. For each pilot in Alaska who is careless, there are hundreds of good ones who carefully obey safety guidelines. The state has nearly eleven thousand registered pilots (one out of every fifty residents) and 7,500 registered aircraft (one for every seventy-three residents). "Alaska has eight times as many pilots, fifteen times as many aircraft and seventy-two times as many commuter aircraft on a per capita basis as the rest of the United States," says the 1988 FAA literature. "Merrill Field (in Anchorage), one of the nation's busiest general aviation airports, records more than three hundred thousand takeoffs and landings each year. Lake Hood, near Anchorage, is the world's largest and busiest seaplane base, accommodating more than eight hundred float plane takeoffs and landings on a peak summer day."

If you drive your car around Lake Hood, you will likely fall in line behind the Pipers, de Havillands, Grummans, and Cessnas taxiing down the road. Alaska has approximately one thousand airstrips, second only to California and Texas (but California and Texas have fifty and thirty times more people, respectively). No wonder Alaska has been called the "flyingest state in the Union." Explains one pilot, "I can't imagine Alaska without flying. It's part of the frontier spirit up here, part of the pride. Take away flying and it just wouldn't be Alaska anymore."

Two F-15s from the Alaska Air Command await takeoff as a Northern Air Cargo DC-6 lands at King Salmon.

The enthusiasm is unbridled. If you tell folks you are writing a book on bush pilots, you will hear responses like: "Really? Hey, there's this guy in Fairbanks you've got to meet. He's got twenty thousand hours in a Cub and he flies like a bird." Or, "I know a pilot in Dutch Harbor who's kind of nervous on the ground, fidgeting around, but once he's in the air at the controls he's another person—relaxed, smiling, having a good time. It's like he was born to fly." Or, "You gotta go flying with this guy. He's got a sticker in his plane that says, 'Where the road ends, the real Alaska begins.'" Or, "Kim, I gotta tell ya, there's this great pilot in Eagle, he's not flamboyant or nothin', he's just real steady and dependable and friendly—kind of the quiet type—but I think he'd be honored to be in your book." Or, "Look, Kim, you'd be crazy not to interview this guy. He's one of the finest individuals I've ever met. He's got four planes, and do you know who he named them after? His wife and three daughters. I'll bet if he ran for mayor he'd win." And so it goes. It seems everyone who has flown in small planes in Alaska has a favorite pilot.

Within the ranks of the U. S. Department of the Interior fly a special breed of pilots who keep one eye on the controls and the other on wildlife. "We call them 'dual function' pilots," says Bruce Batten, who is the assistant regional director for public affairs with the Alaska Region of the U. S. Fish and Wildlife Service. "Some are biologists or refuge managers who census birds and collar caribou, wolves, polar bears, and walruses. Others are law enforcement specialists who stake out suspected poachers. Mike Spindler, for example, assistant manager at the Selawik National Wildlife Refuge, flies a Super Cub out of Kotzebue and has developed a skill for tracking polar bears and landing on the frozen Chukchi Sea. The last time I was up with him, we landed in the middle of the sea ice when it was twenty-five degrees below zero. Our sandwiches froze in an instant. Mike put his hands in the engine cowling to keep them warm."

Batten also talks about Bruce Conant who flies a one-of-a-kind Garrett-powered turboprop Beaver out of Juneau.

"He counts migratory waterfowl by flying transects 100 feet off the ground at 100 mph. The extra power is important to suddenly pull out of danger. In the winter he flies to Mexico to count birds in their wintering habitat. All these guys are remarkable. Put them together in one room and you should hear the stories they tell. They don't have that cocky *Top Gun* attitude. They're extremely competent, but also soft-spoken and humble and levelheaded. It's the right stuff for flying in Alaska."

Much has changed since the earliest birdmen scaled the skies of Alaska nearly three-quarters of a century ago. They, too, in their own way, had the right stuff. But what might they think of Alaskan aviation today? Of helicopters carrying cruise ship tourists from Juneau to the Mendenhall Glacier? Of Alaska Airlines, one of the more successful national carriers, with its forty-eight hundred full-time employees, fifty-one jets, and routes stretching from Prudhoe Bay to Puerto Vallarta (plus two recent friendship flights to the USSR to reunite families from Alaska and Siberia that have been separated for generations)? What might they think of today's commercial bush pilots' spending weeks writing those required operations manuals and filling out the FAA forms in duplicate and triplicate—of the sight of a Grumman Goose, a MarkAir Boeing 737, and a Piper PA-23 Aztec waiting for King Salmon tower clearance after an F-15 lands?

Perhaps they would smile and say, "Pack a lunch, let's go flying. Aviation ain't what she used to be, but Alaska is." The mountains, fjords, and tundra, the glaciers and wildlife—they steal your heart away. No wonder Noel Wien said, "It tugs at you all the time." Once you have flown the Last Frontier, face it, you are spoiled.

So, you see, all along I have known that my nephew, Rob, who at nineteen saw a Cessna 206 land like poetry on glass-still water in Glacier Bay, would come back. And he has known it, too.

Right: Temsco Helicopters' Aerospatiale AStar 350B hovers over the Mendenhall Glacier. Flightseeing is big with cruise ship passengers.

In late afternoon, cumulus clouds backlight a Cessna 206 flying above the Lynn Canal in Southeast Alaska.

■ *Left:* A break in cloud cover reveals rugged slopes of the Coast Range as Wings of Alaska's Cessna 206 follows open waters of the Inside Passage. Flying on floats allows Southeast Alaskan pilots choices of myriad landing opportunities should visibility fall below safe minimums. ■ *Above:* Clear skies reveal that the Southeast Panhandle contains its share of Alaska's spectacular scenery. ■ *Overleaf:* Bush planes parked at St. Cloud Aviation's yard in Anchorage await maintenance.

■ *Above:* Most climbers of 20,306-foot Denali fly to the 7,200-foot base camp on Kahiltna Glacier's Southeast Fork. ■ *Right:* Howard Bowman flies his Stinson Voyager 108 with a PDX conversion from his gold mine above Lake Clark to Port Alsworth for mail. ■ *Following page:* Alaska Airlines has grown from bush flying to a major international carrier. A Wings of Alaska Beaver and an Alaska Airlines Boeing 737 race for the cut. The Beaver gracefully defers to the Boeing 737.

■ *Left:* A Super Cub from Meekin's Flying Service descends for a ski landing on Grizzly Lake high in the Chugach Mountains. ■ *Above:* Flying in Alaska is much safer today than early in the bush pilot era. However, mishaps can still occur. Here, an Otter's left gear caught soft snow causing the plane to career off the Bonanza Hills strip. Except for damaged pride, no one was injured. After three days of field repairs, the Otter was flown to Soldotna for a complete overhaul.

With parallel airstrips plus Hardenburg Bay, wheel and float planes are provided access to the village of Port Alsworth on Lake Clark. Both strips are privately owned. Pilots use the radio frequency 122.9 megahertz to announce their intentions. With a population of only fifty permanent residents, a busy summer afternoon can still find bush planes stacked up waiting to land. The community supports five fishing lodges and is field headquarters for Lake Clark National Park.

Chapter Two

ANYWHERE YOU'LL RIDE, I'LL FLY

by Kim Heacox

A YS-11A belonging to Reeve Aleutian Airways visits the village of Sand Point in the Shumagin Islands.

It is said old bush pilots are like old soldiers; they do not die, they just fade away. Their stories live on and become the stuff of legends. Aviation in Alaska has changed significantly. Things pilots did fifty years ago would cost them their licenses today. But the human spirit endures, the wilderness remains, and no book on Alaskan bush pilots would be complete without one of the great old stories.

Early in 1937, the New England Museum of Natural History organized an expedition to Alaska, headed by Bradford Washburn, to scale 17,147-foot Mount Lucania, then the highest unclimbed peak in North America. Getting there would be a formidable task, for Lucania lay in the remote, frozen heart of the Saint Elias Range in the far southwest corner of Yukon Territory, where access would be practical by plane only. Obviously, Washburn needed a pilot, but not just any pilot. He wrote to Bob Reeve.

The letter carefully detailed everything Washburn would need: a supply flight to carry gear and cache it on the Walsh Glacier, beneath Mount Lucania, then two more flights (several weeks later) to carry four climbers (two per flight) and more gear. Every glacier landing would be at approximately 8,500 feet, higher than any fully loaded ski plane had ever landed.

"Can you do it?" Washburn asked at the end of his letter.

Days passed. Finally a telegram arrived from Bob Reeve with one laconic line: "Anywhere you'll ride, I'll fly."

Washburn was astounded. "You have no idea what a delightful shock that was. No answer to my letter, no discussion, no details. Just that simple statement. I started making my plans for the expedition immediately."

Russell Dow, one of Washburn's climbing partners, traveled to Valdez in March with the expedition's supplies. Reeve and Dow then transported the supplies in Reeve's single-engine Fairchild 71 to a snow landing at McCarthy, the halfway point. From there they ferried the gear in lighter loads to base camp on the Walsh Glacier. Upon landing the first time, Reeve breathed a sign of relief. His altimeter read 8,750 feet. A leaned fuel mixture running through his Wright engine powered the Fairchild as well at 8,750 feet

as at sea level. Despite large crevasses upslope and downslope, and an abnormally low snowfall in the Saint Elias Mountains that winter, the spring snow was still solid; conditions were good. Reeve and Dow made two more trips from McCarthy to Walsh Glacier, cached the climbing gear and returned to Valdez.

Everything was set, but the rest of the climbers did not arrive in Valdez until early June, and poor weather pinned them down for another week. Snow was melting rapidly at lower elevations. The high base camp might still be solid and good for landing, but McCarthy was out. Between Valdez and Walsh Glacier—240 miles of rugged terrain through the Chugach and Saint Elias Mountains—there would be no place to land safely or refuel.

Two years earlier, Wiley Post and Will Rogers had died in a plane crash near Barrow. And six years before that, in 1929, Carl Ben Eielson had augered his Hamilton into the snows of Siberia, killing himself and his mechanic, Earl Borland. "I have a feeling," Borland had said before he and Eielson left Teller, "that we'll never come home." He was right. To this day, some folks say Eielson was an overrated pilot, while others say he was the best. He had received the Distinguished Flying Cross and the Harmon Trophy, and like Post and Rogers, had befriended everyone he met. And now all three were dead. America was getting tired of losing her heroes in air crashes in Alaska.

Like others in Alaska's *esprit de corps* of early birdmen—Eielson, the Wien brothers, Joe Crosson, Harold Gillam, Jack Jefford, Archie Ferguson, Frank Barr—Bob Reeve came to the north poor in pocketbook but rich in heart. In the finest tradition of Americana, he was fiercely independent; a tall, dark, and handsome man; a likable, quick-witted, shoot-from-the-lip, seat-of-the-pants flier whom once you met, you never forgot. And he flew like an eagle. He left home a runaway and arrived in Alaska a stowaway, but in the intervening years made his mark in South America by flying the Pan American-Grace Airways mail run between Santiago in Chile and Lima in Peru, crossing wild latitudes of jungle, pampas, volcanoes, and glaciers. In 1930 alone,

Red salmon are loaded into containers for a fifteen-minute flight across Kvichak Bay to Naknek canneries.

he flew 1,476 hours—then a world record. He returned to the States a wealthy man, but squandered it all. "I'd earned money like a horse," he said, "but I spent it like a jack-ass."

In the summer of 1932, as a freighter pulled up to Valdez, Alaska, Bob Reeve slipped out from under a tarpaulin covering and made for shore with two dollars in his pocket. He located a wrecked Eaglerock biplane, patched it up for part-time work, then bought it, cleared airstrips from a cow pasture and a tide flat, and opened for business. "Always Use Reeve Airways," announced the sign painted on his shed hanger. "Slow Unreliable Unfair and Crooked. Scared and Unlicensed and Nuts. Reeve Airways—the Best." He did not write it, but neither did he erase it.

His reputation as the "glacier pilot" spread quickly across the country, due largely to writer Rex Beach's descriptions of his flying exploits in *Cosmopolitan* and *American* magazines. Readers discovered his routine of flying miners into unmapped terrain, landing his plane on skis on remote glaciers, and using those same skis to land back in the mud in Valdez. Fan mail poured in, most of it from women with matrimony on their minds. But Reeve, a confirmed bachelor, had better things to do. Why ponder the purple prose of some lonely woman when you have a plane to fly?

Then one caught him. "Of all the letters I'd gotten," he said, "I think this is the only one I really read through. It was gay, funny. It sparkled with personality." It was from Janice Morisette in a small town in Wisconsin, not far from where Bob had been raised. She asked if he needed "a secretary, bookkeeper or extra mine hand?" They wrote back and forth for three months and Janice finally responded, "I've booked passage to Alaska. Will arrive Valdez June 19."

Reeve was horrified. A woman coming to Alaska to find *him!* He immediately flew to Canada to mine for gold. Janice arrived, found no Bob Reeve, and took a secretarial job at the Road Commission office. A month later, flooded with curiosity and guilt, Reeve flew back to Valdez. "She sure is cute," a friend told him when he arrived. That afternoon, they walked into town and got a peek at Janice through the Road Commission office window. She was

cute, all right, and efficient. Said Reeve: "Punching that ole typewriter with her black hair and all, she reminded me of Tillie the Toiler." He was sorry he had not returned to Valdez sooner. A year later, Bob and "Tillie" were married.

On June 18, 1937, Reeve slogged across the muddy strip in Valdez and loaded his Fairchild with 350 pounds of equipment and extra gas (for the return trip). If everything went right, he would have just enough fuel to get to Mount Lucania and back. And if something went wrong, well, he would talk with God and look for a place to land. Washburn and another mountaineer, Robert Bates, climbed in. The Fairchild roared down the field, splashed through the mud and lifted ponderously into the air, eastbound.

A thirty-knot headwind blew. It took two hours to reach the halfway point where an important decision had to be made, for to continue on meant there would be no turning back. Reeve considered his options, glanced at his passengers and pushed on. "You know," he yelled above the screaming engine, "if you turn back that first time, you're liable to find yourself doing it over and over."

The land was his map. He flew through the Chugach Range and up the Chitina River past peopleless valleys and nameless mountains memorized on previous runs. Reeve studied the weather and worked the controls, flying just below the strongest winds at six thousand feet. The Fairchild was lighter; half of the fuel in the tank had been burned. There were no runways below, or farms or fields. Only ice, rock, forests, rivers—wilderness. Pilots with thousands of hours flying over the Midwest had come to Alaska to fly over this wilderness, and had failed. In the entire Alaska Territory in 1937 there existed not one federal paved airstrip, lighted field, or radio beacon.

Since 1923, when Ben Eielson had first climbed into the wicker seat and open cockpit of his World War I Curtiss Jenny and lifted off a baseball field in Fairbanks, more than one-third of the planes in Alaska had been destroyed. Granted, there were many accidents—sixty-three pilots and passengers would die in Alaska in the decade prior to World War II—but in that same decade more than thirty

Captain John Spencer pilots Reeve's YS-11A above the Alaska Peninsula.

million miles would be flown through the wild Alaskan skies. Noel Wien, a quiet man with a reputation for understatement, mused, "We flew without radio and without weather reports over unmapped mountains in the worst weather that God inflicts on this earth." In her book, *The Flying North,* Jean Potter writes, "bush pilots are the flyingest people under the American flag and probably . . . in the world. By 1939, the small airlines of the [Alaska] Territory were hauling twenty-three times as many passengers and a thousand times as much freight, per capita, as the rest of the U. S."

It was not easy. Joe Crosson, famous for his searches for Eielson, Post, and Rogers, said flying the Arctic in winter was like "flying inside a milk bottle." Other pilots said the combination of wind, fog, and topography in Southeast Alaska was the worst. Reports of hundred-mile-an-hour winds and fog hundreds of feet thick came from the Alaska Peninsula and the Aleutian Islands. People out there joked about the day the wind stopped blowing and everybody fell down. Yet there was, and is, no place in Alaska so inspiring and intimidating with mountains, glaciers, and icefields as the Wrangell-Saint Elias region, the heart of which Reeve, Washburn, and Bates were now entering.

Reeve flew past the headwaters of the Chitina River and over the dirty, jumbled snout of the Logan Glacier. "Till my dying day," Washburn remembered, "I shall never forget that nauseating desolation of dying masses of ice . . . veneered with a deep layer of reddish boulders and gravel. The valley walls on both sides were vertical rock and scree, bare, snowless and bleak. Potholes of horrid muddy water filled every depression. . . ."

Reeve was smoking like a chimney. "He had that inseparable rainhat pulled down over his ears," according to Washburn, "and his cigarette holder clamped between his teeth. Every few seconds, he'd hold the stick with his knees, while he took his pocket knife and flipped the butt out of the holder, then crammed in a fresh cigarette."

Finally, Walsh Glacier came into view beneath a sullen sky, and on it a small, black dot: the cache. Although winds had buffeted the plane, now, at an elevation of nine thousand feet, it was dead calm as Reeve made his approach. Dark clouds hemmed in from above, the deeply-crevassed glacier from below. Reeve lowered the nose, the plane began to drop. "Flying into that valley was like entering a tunnel with a dead end," Washburn said. "A mile on either side of us almost vertical cliffs of ice and rock rose into the clouds. Below us tossed the rough surface of our glacier. Seven or eight miles ahead the valley floor and walls melted into the murky ceiling, the lower surfaces of which we were just skimming. Behind us the storm was dropping down. He [Reeve] used the black slits of open crevasses to come in safely. He throttled back the motor and dropped steeply to a point in the middle of the cracks. With the stabilizer slightly tail-heavy and the motor idle, we dropped at a fast rate. About fifty feet above the crevasses, Bob gave the motor full throttle and pulled sharply back the stick. He cleared all the cracks but the last little ones; the tails of the skis touched these and we settled to a perfect three-point landing in the snow a dozen yards beyond."

But the surface of Walsh Glacier was more slush than snow. Washburn jumped out and sank to his waist. Reeve quickly refueled the plane, turned it around using ropes and the help of the two climbers, and tried to take off. But after sloshing along for only fifty yards and burning up valuable fuel, the Fairchild hit a soft spot and sank to its wingtips. Reeve was stuck. For the next four days, he probably aged four years as foggy, rainy, warm weather stranded him on the glacier with Washburn and Bates. Several times he tried to taxi his plane to firmer ground only to sink in the slush again to a wingtip. So again he dug the Fairchild out and waited.

The expedition was doomed. Reeve would be unable to fly in the other two climbers—Russell Dow and Norman Bright—or to return to get Washburn and Bates. They would have to walk out. Come to think of it, Reeve would also have to walk out, abandoning his plane, if the glacial surface did not refreeze so he could fly out. At one point, when Washburn invited him to climb to a cache he and Bates had

An Otter leased by Diamond Aviation of Wrangell unloads fuel at Johnny Mountain Gold Mine airstrip.

established another thousand feet up the glacier, Reeve wrapped himself in his sleeping bag, hunkered down in the tiny tent next to his plane and snarled, "I'm a pilot, not a mountain climber. You skin your skunks and I'll skin mine."

The fifth morning dawned cool and foggy, but clear overhead. A thin crust of newly formed ice covered the glacier. Washburn and Bates helped Reeve turn the plane into the sun to melt frost off the wings and tail. Reeve flattened the propeller with a wrench to maximize horsepower. A disturbing ten-mile-per-hour wind blew down the glacier—the direction he needed to taxi. Downslope, the glacier dropped into a chasm surrounded by vertical rock walls. The fog began to lift and the three men glanced at each other. It was now or never. Reeve climbed in, wearing his leather jacket and oil-stained pants, waved stoically and prepared to either fly or die.

"I gave it the gun and off I went. But . . . I hadn't gone a hundred feet when smack! down into a crevasse. But I wasn't stopping. The engine was developing tremendous power, far beyond its rated capacity. I climbed right out of the crevasse and kept going. Then flop! down into another—and I'd lost the air speed I'd gained, getting out of it. Bumpety bump, it was just like driving over a plowed road. I realized I was getting nowhere. I'd already run a mile or more, and ahead of me I could see the big crevasses— wide enough to hold a boxcar. If I hit them, I was a goner. Then I happened to glance left and spotted an icefall sheering off the side—maybe a 250-foot drop. It was my last chance. I made a sharp left turn and dove the plane right over that icefall. It mushed straight for the bottom, and I thought maybe I was a goner after all. But the plane had achieved just enough forward speed on the jump-over to become air-borne. I leveled out about ten feet from the bottom. That was the greatest feeling of my life—bar none!"

And from Washburn's perspective: "I never hope to see wings hop and jerk and lunge back and forth the way that old plane did. Halfway down the runway she still jerked. She had no speed, and her tail was still on the snow, bouncing up and down over each drift. I was just about to

turn to Bates and say, 'She's all up, we'll have to tramp down a runway,' when Reeve suddenly turned the plane sharply to the left, down a steep sidehill leading toward an awful mass of cracks and a little greenish lake on the south side of the valley. There was a last roar and he disappeared out of sight. We could hear the 'rrrr' of the motor. We waited for the crash. There was silence. Bates and I both thought we'd never in God's world get her out of that hole. Then suddenly we heard the rasping roar of the engine, and the plane came into sight going like fury in front of the lake, and heading triumphantly for Logan, a black speck against the snow. Bates and I were simply spellbound. That steep hill had given Bob Reeve what he needed. It was a desperate maneuver which for almost any other pilot would have been suicidal. We shrieked for joy."

Reeve made it back to Valdez with no fuel to spare. "For five cents I would have dropped a lighted match in either gas tank," he said. Tillie jumped in the old Model T and raced down to greet him. Washburn and Bates managed to not only walk out of the Saint Elias Mountains to the settlement of Burwash Landing, in the Yukon, but to scale Mount Lucania as well. Years later, Washburn, himself a pilot, would hail Reeve as "without a doubt the finest ski pilot and rough country flyer I've seen."

Twenty years later, Bob Reeve would be on top of the world with Tillie and their five children, Richard, Roberta, Janice, David, and Whitty, and his own congressionally certified airline company, Reeve Aleutian Airways, with a spotless safety record and planes flying to the farthest corners of the land. "Mr. Alaska," friends would say upon introducing him in the Lower 48.

He was one of a kind. Yet Bob Reeve would insist that others were as equally accomplished, and that although much has changed over the decades, flying in Alaska continues to give today what it gave back then—a chance to grow, to be alive, to live a dream.

Right: Ellen Paneok, a pilot for Cape Smythe Air in Barrow, tends one of her antique aircraft—a restored Fairchild 24-J—in Wasilla.

■ *Left:* Andy Greenblatt of Brooks Range Aviation lands his Piper PA-18 Super Cub along the Koyukuk River's North Fork. Ideal for short field work, Andy's Cub can take off in 250 to 300 feet. ■ *Above:* An extremely popular plane in Alaska, a Super Cub's greenhouse canopy and tandem seating provide excellent visibility.

■ *Above:* Leon Alsworth flies his Taylorcraft BC-12-D over Lake Clark's Chulitna Bay. ■ *Right:* Jimmy Branham's Waco YKC is one of the only two left in the world on floats. This 1934 biplane began its flying career in Alaska in 1937 with pilot Red Flensburg at Dillingham Air Service. After ten years of service around the Bristol Bay area, the Waco was sold to the Branham family at Rainy Pass Lodge. The Branhams sold the plane in 1956 but repurchased it for restoration in 1973.

■ *Left:* National Park Ranger Larry Van Slyke helps pull a Cessna 185 from Lake Clark. Luckily, the pilot and passengers escaped injury. ■ *Above:* Weighing more than 350 pounds, a drum of jet fuel makes quite a splash when rolled from Sound Adventure's Twin Otter. The fuel will keep Temsco Helicopter's Hughes 500 flying during work for the U. S. Geological Survey. ■ *Overleaf:* Barbara Shallcross takes flightseers over Glacier Bay National Park in Haines Airways' Piper Cherokee 180.

Pilot Mike Reynolds and gold miner Phil Barr bag a husky for transport.

■ *Above:* Sled dogs check both the pilot and Lake Clark Air Service's Cessna 206 before embarking on an hour-long trip. Burlap sacks curtail dog fights in the air.
■ *Right:* One of Alaska's more than five thousand private pilots, Alan White flies his Cessna 185 above the braided channels of the Knik and Matanuska rivers.

Chapter Three

THE DENALI FLYERS

by Kim Heacox

The dispatcher for Talkeetna Air Taxi, Kathleen Fleming gives Barney a hug.

The highest mountain in North America has two names: McKinley and Denali. The first honors William McKinley, the twenty-fifth president of the United States. The second comes from the Athabascans of Interior Alaska and respectfully means "the High One." Because the U. S. Board on Geographic Names recognizes the name McKinley, not Denali, many Alaskans refuse to recognize the U. S. Board on Geographic Names.

Denali, the crown of the continent, rises 20,306 feet above sea level, head and shoulders over all surrounding peaks in the Alaska Range. More than a mountain, it is a massif, a great granitic bulge covered year-round in ice and snow. Captain George Vancouver saw it in 1794 from 120 miles to the south in Knik Arm from the deck of HMS *Discovery.* Early Russian explorers made special note of it, and by the turn of the century, American scientists had determined it was North America's highest peak.

Mountaineers around the world took notice. But it was Hudson Stuck, an archdeacon from Nenana, who led the first successful summit climb in 1913. "I remember no day in my life so full of toil, distress and exhaustion," he wrote, "and yet so full of happiness and keen gratification." Since then, Denali has attracted a steady stream of would-be conquerors. By 1988, approximately 10,300 had attempted the climb, 5,500 had succeeded, and 60 had died.

For the thrill of a lifetime—standing on top of North America—hundreds of climbers test their mettle on those icy slopes each year, gambling against hypoxia, high altitude sickness, nausea, and frostbite—the same conditions encountered by Stuck. But instead of walking from the surrounding lowlands as he did, most climbers today take a less footsore, more Jovian route. They fly by ski plane to 7,200 feet on the Kahiltna Glacier, a thrill in itself. For flying the ski planes are some of the best glacier pilots in the world—Lowell Thomas, Jr., Doug Geeting, Cliff Hudson, and Jim Okonek—commonly called the Denali flyers.

Left: Wheel-skis allow the versatility of taking off and landing on pavement in Talkeetna and on the snow and ice of Denali's glaciers.

The adventure begins in rustic Talkeetna, population 250 on a sunny day, elevation 350 feet every day. "Beautiful Downtown Talkeetna," reads the sign as you enter town. Quiet most of the year, Talkeetna explodes into an international mountaineering mecca during May and June as climbers from Japan, Korea, Scotland, Germany, France, Canada, Mexico, Switzerland, the United States, and a dozen other countries arrive to scale North America's greatest prize, whimsically called "the hill" by the pilots, sixty air miles to the north-northwest. After checking in with park rangers, the climbers head for the airstrip.

An hour later, they are staring at the Alaska Range and "the hill." The plane drones in the alpine ether, as sunlight dances off ice, rock, and snow. Serrated ridges scythe the horizon. Crevasses slice the glaciers. A climber asks how the pilot finds his way when the clouds roll in. "Good hunches," he says, "and an occasional glimpse of a familiar peak or ridge." The plane zips on past Avalanche Spire, through One Shot Pass, and down on the Kahiltna Glacier, a river of ice three miles wide and forty-seven miles long. After unloading climbers and gear, the pilot loads up another team to return to Talkeetna. And so it goes on sunny spring days from 5:00 a.m. to 11:00 p.m. as the skies between Talkeetna and Denali buzz with Cessnas, Super Cubs, and Helio Couriers.

"This is some of the most interesting, challenging, and wonderful flying anywhere," says Jim Okonek, owner of K₂ Aviation. "Jacques Cousteau's pilot wrote to me once for a job. Pilots from everywhere have asked about working here." Aside from mountaineers, the Talkeetna pilots also fly hunters, fishermen, and other passengers. "You never can tell what might come along," Okonek says. He once flew a photographer and a woman onto a glacier, where the woman disrobed for *Playboy's* "Women of Alaska."

Flying his turbo-charged Helio Courier around Denali, Lowell Thomas, Jr., the owner of Talkeetna Air Taxi, has landed as high as 14,200 feet to make rescues. In 1984, he experienced one of his "most touching moments" when he flew a Japanese camera crew to Denali to monitor the

Base Camp manager Norma Jean Saunders pulls equipment to K₂ Aviation's Cessna 185 on Kahiltna Glacier.

progress of climber Naomi Uemura. "We saw him briefly through the clouds and spoke with him by CB radio as he closed in on the summit," Thomas says. "Then the clouds rolled in. We spoke with him the next day on his way down. He was somewhere around seventeen thousand feet, and that was the last anyone ever heard from him."

The sadness of Uemura's disappearance softened four years later, when Thomas flew to the mountain in March 1988 to pick up Vern Tejas who attained what Uemura had attempted—the first winter solo ascent of Denali. "When I got up there," Thomas says, "Vern was just a little black dot on the glacier, but he was there alright, and I knew he had made it. I literally let out a whoop for joy, and got him out of there as quickly as possible. You know, flying in Alaska is really not such a hazardous business, provided you go about it in a careful, methodical manner. But if you don't, it's extremely hazardous."

That Alaskan pilots would someday land on glaciers was inevitable—given the state has thousands of glaciers covering twenty-nine thousand square miles (an area roughly the size of South Carolina). But that they would perfect the task into an art—today a *de rigueur* exercise in mountain flying, landing as high as fourteen thousand feet—is an aviation hallmark. Joe Crosson ushered in the era in 1932 by landing his Fairchild on Muldrow Glacier on Denali's northeast side. Others tried and died, but Crosson made repeated landings without mishap. Five years later, Bob Reeve was developing success at glacier flying. Like Crosson, he flew Fairchilds with large, wooden skis, but Reeve added stainless steel bottoms to his skis, enabling landings not only on glaciers but also on muddy fields and tidal flats.

In June of 1951, Terris Moore, pilot, mountaineer, and the new president of the University of Alaska, made the first landings on the Kahiltna Glacier. But rather than using fixed, wooden skis, he outfitted his Super Cub with retractable aluminum skis that enabled him to take off on wheels, then lower the skis into position by using a hydraulic pump installed in the plane's cabin. Moore carried important cargo that year: a climbing party from the Boston Museum

of Science and the University of Denver, headed by pre-eminent mountaineer Bradford Washburn. A month later, Washburn and party were back on the Kahiltna where Moore picked them up at just over ten thousand feet. They had successfully completed the first ascent of Denali by the West Buttress, a route previously thought unclimbable, and today is the safest and most popular way up the mountain.

A scientist and mountaineer, Washburn had many projects he wanted to accomplish. Obviously, he needed a skilled glacier pilot to fly year after year into the cold empyrean of the Alaska Range. Terris Moore was out; he had a university to run. But in August 1951, Washburn met Don Sheldon. "I've heard a lot about that kid," Bob Reeve told his old friend, Washburn, "and he's either crazy and is going to kill himself, or he'll turn out to be one . . . good pilot." Indeed, not only did Don Sheldon become one of Alaska's greatest pilots and one of the original Denali flyers, he also married Bob Reeve's daughter, Roberta.

"Not even the most inventive adventure-fiction writer could improve on some of Sheldon's exploits," claims the back cover of *Wager With the Wind, The Don Sheldon Story,* by James Greiner. Referring to 1955, Greiner wrote, "The year was only partially over and already Sheldon had done more mountain flying and made more risky landings than many pilots do in a lifetime." Among his many exploits that spring: he airdropped a bucket of fried chicken to a team of climbers who had run out of food and subsisted on lemon drops for five days, and he flew a layered cake and canned peaches in for Washburn who was mapping the Ruth Amphitheater on Denali's south side. But that July, Sheldon made two of his most memorable rescues.

In the first, a plane crashed into the Talkeetna River and the pilot stumbled into town early the next morning with a knot on his head and said, "I don't know if the passengers got out or not. I hope they haven't drowned." Sheldon immediately flew his Super Cub east up the river through the early morning rain. Approaching the crash site, he could not believe his eyes, for on a sand bar in the middle of the river stood a 300-pound lady, frantically waving her

Lowell Thomas, Jr., has landed his Helio Courier at elevations as high as 14,200 feet on Denali's glaciers.

arms. She was naked! "Naked as a jaybird," Sheldon said. "She would have been hard to miss, even in the poor light of a rainy morning." He airdropped her a sleeping bag, returned to Talkeetna to wait for better light, then flew back for the rescue, landing on the river and drifting downstream to pick her up. She was alone; the other passenger had made it to town. The lady was the proprietress of the Fairbanks Hotel, and once back in the Fairview Inn in Talkeetna she regaled everyone who would listen with stories of the experience.

Sheldon's second rescue that month was not so comical. A detachment of eight U. S. Army scouts planned to raft through treacherous Devil's Canyon on the Susitna River, sixty-five miles upstream of Talkeetna. A couple of days after their departure, Sheldon flew his Aeronca Sedan over the canyon to monitor their progress. All he saw were pieces of yellow raft and cans of gas floating downstream. Not a good sign. Finally, he sighted the scouts huddled on a ledge next to a vertical rock wall and white-water rapids five feet high. It was impossible to land next to them, or downstream either, for the water was too rough. But a quarter mile upstream he found a stretch of flat water.

"Sheldon was landing against a current of thirty miles per hour, and the airplane decelerated at an alarming rate," wrote Greiner, also a pilot, in Sheldon's biography. "When an airplane is moving through the air at an airspeed of 90 to 100 miles per hour, the control surfaces—ailerons, rudder, and elevator—work at optimum efficiency. . . . An airplane out of its design element and on the ground or water is much more difficult to control. . . . In addition, an airplane on floats is infinitely less maneuverable than one on wheels or even on skis, and as a result, the Aeronca became an unresponsive death trap as it almost immediately began to accelerate downriver with the current."

"The nose wanted to swing in about every imaginable direction." Sheldon said, "But somehow I managed to keep it pointed upriver with the throttle. I was floating backward at about twenty-five miles an hour, the windows were fogged, and I couldn't see where I was going." Then came

the rapids. The plane lurched. Water beat the struts and rolled up to the wingtips. Sheldon throttled forward and inched toward the canyon wall. Suddenly out the side window he saw seven soldiers staring at him in disbelief. He powered the Aeronca up to the ledge, angled the wingtip just off the rock wall and balanced the throttle against the current. One of the scouts jumped onto a float and balance-walked to the cabin. Now what? To taxi upriver was out of the question; the current was too strong, the rapids too big. So Sheldon floated backward a mile and a half, maneuvering the plane with every trick he could muster, until he hit flat water out of the canyon, turned downstream, and took off. Once was a miracle, but he repeated this scenario thrice, each time successfully carrying out two more GIs. Then he searched for, found, and rescued the eighth man, who had clung to debris and floated eighteen miles below the canyon.

For twenty-seven years, Sheldon flew out of Talkeetna, averaging eight hundred hours a year. He went through forty-five airplanes but never harmed a passenger or himself. Once when two hunters from Los Angeles were unable to pay for a flight, he told them, "Heck, that's okay. When you get back to L. A. make the money and send it to me."

The hunters were dumbfounded. "You mean you would trust us to leave, owing you this money?"

"Oh for Pete's sake," Sheldon said, "I can tell you are good, honest guys."

Don Sheldon died of cancer in 1975. He was fifty-four.

I spoke with his wife, Roberta, about all the books and articles written about him, and about her father and the other great Alaskan pilots. I asked, "Is there anything that's never been said that you'd like to say now?"

"Well," she replied, "these people are famous for their skills and their daring rescues, but they were also human beings, sometimes exceptional human beings in their humanity. Don was such a person. He was a good, kind man. That's what touched me most—his humanity. But in the context of a book, well, I don't know. I suppose it just doesn't fit."

■ *Left:* Just caught in Help-Me-Jack Lake in the Brooks Range, this lake trout in male spawning colors is proudly displayed by fisherman Tyler Klaes, age nine. Having a bush pilot for a father helps in finding the best angling spots. ■ *Above:* Glassy waters of Icy Strait reflect a spectacular sunset as a Cessna 206 flies toward Pleasant Island, Glacier Bay, and the Fairweather Range. Glacier Bay National Park is a popular destination for cruise ships, sightseeing flights, and kayak trips.

■ *Above:* Water flies from a puddle on the McKinley Park strip as Bran-Air Pilot Don Glaser takes off in a Piper Super Cub. Antennas attached to the plane's wing struts assist biologists in tracking radio-collared wolves, moose, and caribou in Denali National Park. ■ *Right:* A hazy sun silhouettes a Beaver on amphibious floats owned by O.A.S. of the U. S. Department of the Interior. ■ *Overleaf:* Bush planes return to the Lake Hood Airstrip as a full moon rises above Anchorage.

Wing and tail covers keep lift-destroying snow and frost from accumulating on a tied-down Cessna 170.

■ *Left:* Winter operations require extra efforts to keep engines warm. An engine cover holds heat for a few hours. ■ *Above:* To warm a Cessna 185's engine on an icy morning, Ed Barber uses a portable propane heater. With piston-driven aircraft, most pilots cease flying when temperatures drop between zero and -30 degrees Fahrenheit. Minimum temperatures for turboprop planes are -30 to -50 degrees Fahrenheit. Air service to rural Alaska may cease during the severe cold.

■ *Above:* Salt water landings leave corrosive spray on aircraft aluminum. Pilot Doug Riemer washes one of Alaska Island Air's Cessna 180s in Petersburg.
■ *Right:* Alaska's skies attract a steady parade of new aviators. Ray Halderman won his 1966 Alon Aircoup with a twenty-dollar raffle ticket purchased from the North Star Flying Lions Club. North of the Arctic Circle, he flies with his instructor on a cross-country training flight above the North Fork of the Koyukuk River.

Pilot Price Brower flies the Bell 214 Super Transport in emergency work.

■ *Left:* The ice conditions which trapped three gray whales north of Barrow in the fall of 1988 also wrecked havoc with Arctic Ocean shipping. Cape Smythe Air's de Havilland DHC-6 Twin Otter regularly flew ice reconnaissance patrols in order to monitor the extent and movement of the pack ice. ■ *Above:* North Slope Borough Search and Rescue's Bell 214 Super Transport delivers emergency radio equipment to the vessel, *Big Valley,* trapped by pack ice northwest of Barrow.

■ *Above:* Denali's south face looms above peaks of the Alaska Range and K₂ Aviation's Cessna 185. Ground fog often obscures glacier landing sites. The air taxis that land climbers, skiers, and sightseers on Denali's glaciers routinely swap information on the changeable weather. ■ *Right:* Spectacular, awesome, and forbidding only begin to describe the scenery in Denali National Park. Passengers in a four-place Cessna watch as wispy clouds enshroud a glacier-clad mountain.

Rob Everts balances on his family's metalized 1929 Travelair, one of the state's oldest still-active planes.

■ *Left:* Steep slopes and heavy timber preclude access by conventional aircraft to much of Southeast Alaska's backcountry. An Aerospatiale AStar 350B flies past sheer granite walls. ■ *Above:* Doug Solberg flies over Icy Strait in the United States' last commercially operating Norseman, a plane affectionately called "Thunder Chicken" by Canadian pilots. Over two thousand hours went toward restoring this 1943 Norseman which flew Alaska's North Slope after World War II.

One of four in existence, Trans-Provincial Airline's Twin Engine Bristol flies from Wrangell to British Columbia.

■ *Above:* Michael Branham departs a small lake in Fox Bay Lodge's Turbo Beaver DHC-2 Mark III. Sixty Turbo Beavers were manufactured by de Havilland from 1963 to 1968. ■ *Right:* When cruise ships call on coastal towns, passengers eagerly look forward to viewing spectacular glaciers, waterfalls, and mountains from helicopters and fixed-wing aircraft. Soloy Helicopters' Hughes 500 ends a Columbia Glacier tour with a fly-by of the "Royal Princess" docked in Valdez.

■ *Left:* Temsco Airlines' Beaver pilot-in-training practices turns while step-taxiing on the Behm Canal. ■ *Above:* Smoke flies from the nine cylinders of an Otter's 600-horse radial engine. Before serving Diamond Aviation of Wrangell, this Otter flew with the Greenland Expedition to search for B-17s and P-38s buried in the snow. ■ *Overleaf:* Lake Clark reflects Tanalian Mountain and aircraft used by the National Park Service and Alaska Department of Fish and Wildlife Protection.

■ *Above:* Planes carrying passengers for hire undergo an extensive maintenance check every one hundred hours. Certified Aircraft Mechanic Don Cook begins the check on Bellair's Beaver during a warm and sunny afternoon in Sitka. Plane usage in daylight dictates that mechanics often must work through the wee hours of the night. ■ *Right:* Produce is loaded on a Beaver in Juneau. Customers of Snyder Mercantile in Tenakee Springs eagerly await the weekly fresh food flight.

■ *Left:* Rural Alaskan pilots are good sources for information on the bush. At Bettles Field, hunters crowd around John Hajdukovich's Widgeon to learn of sheep hunting areas in the Brooks Range. ■ *Above:* Hollis Twitchell and Jimmy Balluta swap stories beneath Jimmy's Taylorcraft F-19 prior to a fall caribou hunt in the Koksetna Hills. Alaskan law requires hunters to wait at least until 3 a.m. of the day following the day they have been airborne before commencing hunting.

Pacific Alaska's Fairchild F-27 takes on fuel at the steel runway at Point Barrow, the state's northernmost point.

■ *Above:* Don Nyberg and Dave Henley set up a final approach for Point Barrow. Weather permitting, Pacific Alaska's F-27 regularly services the Arctic Ocean DEW (Defense Early Warning) Line Stations between Point Lay and Barter Island. Fog in summer and severe cold in winter may result in changed flight plans or cancellations. ■ *Right:* Produced by de Havilland Aircraft Company in Canada from 1951 to 1967, the Otter's large tail reminds one of pre-World War II planes.

Chapter Four

DON'T GO THROUGH THE LOOKING GLASS

by Kim Heacox

Air taxis are essential to medivacs. Paramedics remove a patient from Peninsula Airways' Navajo Chieftain.

My telephone rang at 9:00 a.m. "Kim, this is Kirk. Let's go flying." It was early January and 10 degrees Fahrenheit. Pale daylight lurked behind the Chugach Mountains, but the sky was dark, and stars were out. Frost covered the windows.

"What do you think, Kim? It's going to be a bluebird day. I phoned flight service and they're calling for clear and calm. The plane's at Sand Lake. How about if we meet there in an hour and fly down to Homer. I want you to meet Bill de Creeft."

I hesitated only a moment while obligations ran through my head. I had manuscript deadlines to meet, phone calls to make, letters to write. "Okay, I'll be there."

Into my survival pack I threw a sleeping bag, fresh water, extra food, warm clothing, first aid kit, cameras, lenses, film, pens, paper, and a small tape recorder with a microphone. Melanie, my wife, packed me a lunch. I arrived at Sand Lake at 10:00 a.m. Kirk was already there preparing the plane—a Piper Super Cruiser PA-12.

He fired up his MSR multi-fuel stove, fitted two three-foot lengths of stove pipe over it, which he ran up to heat the engine. In motions familiar to every pilot in Alaska, he jostled the wings to loosen the skis (in case they had frozen to the lake surface), then moved flaps, ailerons, horizontal stabilizer, and rudder to check the pulleys and cables. He inserted a plunger into the underside of the fuel tanks and drew out gas to check for water, dirt, or ice. "Just like taking a blood sample," he explained.

Warm light poured across the sky. The lake was frozen solid with a fresh dusting of new snow. Perfect flying conditions. We loaded our survival packs. Kirk threw in a pair of snowshoes, then strapped crosscountry skis and poles to the wing strut. "If you go down in snow and need to get out," he mused, "you'll need these."

A former instructor with the National Outdoor Leadership School and later a manager with his wife Leslie at Chenik Brown Bear Photography Camp across Cook Inlet

Left: A double rainbow terminates behind a pair of Cessna 185s at the largest sea plane base in the world—Lake Hood in Anchorage.

from Homer, Kirk now has his own dental practice and airplane in Anchorage. Kirk approaches flying like everything else—aimed firmly towards excellence. He and Leslie both earned their licenses last year. Get them talking about flying and you cannot shut them up.

"Kim," they had pleaded with me, "If you're going to write a book on Alaskan bush pilots, you've got to talk with Bill de Creeft with Kachemak Air Service in Homer. He's one of the best."

Later that week, the phone rang. "This is Mike McBride with Kachemak Bay Wilderness Lodge in Homer. How'ya doin'? Kirk and Leslie told me you were writing a book about bush pilots and mentioned you might be coming down here to talk with Bill de Creeft. Kim, you have to do it. This guy is fantastic. He's a great Alaskan, a great pilot, and a very intelligent, charming and humble man. He's flown clients to and from my lodge for nearly twenty years. He lived in a tent while he built his log cabin when he first arrived here, and over the years he's evolved as the most reliable pilot around. I know, Kim, there are lots of great bush pilots in Alaska and you can't write about them all. But believe me . . . I've seen many pilots who push too hard, who take chances, who grow over-confident and careless. But not Bill. He's a special kind of man. Think about it."

Kirk and I removed the engine covering and stove. He turned the propeller to prime the engine. We climbed in. Seat belts buckled. Headsets on. "Prop!" he yelled. The engine popped twice, then roared like a lion. "Anchorage Tower, this is Piper seven-eight-six-nine-Hotel. I'm on Sand Lake with info foxtrot. Want to depart to the east at two thousand feet with transponder." In other words, Kirk had listened to the weather, and was ready to fly.

"Six niner-Hotel," came the reply in terse aviator's argot, "squawk zero-one-three-one, advise when airborne."

We took off into the cold dense air. Kirk cleared with the tower and activated the flight plan filed earlier. We climbed to 2,800 feet—the elevation required to fly over Turnagain Arm should the engine fail and we need to glide to safe landing. Patterns of ice filled the fjord. A pastel sunlight

Retractable wing-tip floats lowered, a Grumman G-44 Widgeon lands on Iniakuk Lake in the Brooks Range.

warmed the horizon, capped by clouds like halos over the Kenai Mountains. To the west, Iliamna and Redoubt volcanoes glowed so brilliantly pink you expected Handel's Messiah to fill the firmament. The engine hummed.

An hour later we descended along the Kachemak Bay shore, sailed fifty feet over five moose, none of which even looked up, and landed on Beluga Lake in Homer, a town part fiction and part fact in the radio show "End of the Road," by author Tom Bodett, but definitely home to some of Alaska's most fascinating people: painters, protesters, poets, pundits, philosophers, photographers—and pilots.

Perhaps in his mid-fifties, graying hair cropped short and a beard to match, Bill de Creeft stood on shore with his hands in his pockets. "Glad you made it," he said as he shook my hand. Mike McBride arrived, a picture of fitness and exhuberance as he popped out of his carry-all. Ten minutes later, we were in Bill's barn where he was restoring a 1929 six-passenger Travelair monoplane. Bill walks with a limp, but it does not seem to slow him down.

We followed a well-worn trail to the log cabin Bill and Barbara de Creeft have called home for twenty years. Vintage Alaskan, it immediately put us at ease. Two cats and a dog lay on the floor, pots and pans hung on the walls, and HF and VHF radios crackled near the door. Mike made himself comfortable on the sofa. Bill and I relaxed at the table. Kirk sat crosslegged on the floor while Barbara, Bill's wife, set out a bowl of almonds.

"Well," Bill said slowly, obviously unaccustomed to talking about himself, "I'm leary of books and articles on bush pilots because writers tend to romanticize flying up here and make it seem all 'slam-bang-devil-may-care' kind of flying. And while people may like to read about that, they sure don't want that kind of airplane ride. The guys I admire are the ones who build businesses, fly many years, and get to be old. Pilots impressed people in the early days because they could perform magic. The public didn't know what an airplane could do. Planes would go someplace in minutes where a dog team would take days. Now the only way to do magic is to sneak in and out of some spot where no one else

has been before. You finally get to the limit of what an airplane is capable of, no matter how good you are. Pilots find the limit all the time, but they use up an airplane and sometimes themselves. The saying is, 'Pilots don't need food, they live on love and borrowed time,' which is fun to say but unfortunately it isn't true, because in the end you've got to make a living at it. So you've got pilots risking passengers just to stay in business, fighting weather and so forth, and you've got pilots risking passengers just out of their own pride. I've risked my neck lots of times. You can't fly in this part of the world without doing that if you're going to help people in trouble. But I don't do it with a load of passengers just to make a buck or to boost my pride."

When Bill and Barbara arrived in 1962, Homer had five planes. "There must be thirty or forty now," Bill says. He has operated his own compay—Kachemak Air Service—for twenty-two years, flying 17,000 hours and making three forced landings. "And I've turned around many times."

"I've got an advantage over lots of people because I got hurt really bad when I first came up here before starting my own air service. It was twenty-six years ago and it left me with a steel hip that reminds me every time I put my foot down. You don't have to have an accident to be safe, but I sure learned what it feels like to go into the trees. Everything goes bad in a second. It's like going through the looking glass. Suddenly it shatters, and you're on the other side of what you'd always thought was real. If you live through something like that, it's pure chance. It doesn't take long to get to a point beyond which you no longer have control. The weather and the country don't care what a great person you think you are. If you're above clouds and over mountains, or over water so rough you can't land on it, and the engine quits. Bang! It's just a piece of iron that could care less what a swell person you are."

Suddenly he caught himself and drew back. "Good grief, this is turning into a speech. But it's a good chance to spout off, I guess." We nodded, hoping he would continue. One of the cats sprang up, pawed my tape recorder, and jumped onto the windowsill.

A cardiologist in the morning and an air taxi operator in the afternoon, Dr. Gary Archer chats from his Otter.

"I used to fly," Mike said, "but no more. If you want to be a commercial bush pilot, I think you have to ask yourself some hard-nosed questions about motives and abilities. You have to know yourself and your limitations and make yourself live by those limitations—the kind of thing that isn't in any books. I'm not like Bill in having the ability to analyze split-second situations. I could see flying wasn't for me. I got out and I'm glad I did." Today, Mike and his wife, Diane, own and operate Kachemak Bay Wilderness Lodge, one of Alaska's finest. "It's important, too," he added, "that lodge owners like me not pressure pilots like Bill to fly in bad conditions."

Bill smiled. "It's no good explaining accidents by saying the country is rough and the weather is bad. That's the whole point. That's the job. You've got to be better than the country and the weather. Not tougher, just smarter. There are air taxis that fly safely every day. Pilots don't have to scare themselves. They have a choice. If the people you're flying for don't do it right, leave 'em. One day a guy called me and said, 'Flying for this outfit is nerve-wracking. The plane's always overloaded, and I'm always over water in low weather on wheels.'

"I said, 'Have you got a car?'

"'Yeah,' he said, 'it's parked right here.'

"'Well,' I said, 'Why don't you just get in it and drive away from there?'

"Flying up here is a lot of fun, as long as you can do it right. But sometimes the biggest problem is with the passengers. They open the phone book, pick out the air taxi that charges the least . . . not thinking in terms of safety or reliability. Back in the early days, the passengers were local guys—miners or trappers—and they knew who to go with. They would even help sweep snow off the wings if they were stuck a few days. Now it's tourists and they're on an airline schedule, going to places an airline wouldn't touch. It's tougher for a young pilot to stand up to them."

He related a story of a friend in another town who was approached by a lady who wanted to go to Anchorage immediately. "She insisted he take her, even though the weather was terrible, and if he couldn't take her, she'd find somebody who would. 'Look, lady,' he told her, 'There's my gun. Why don't you just step outside and shoot yourself, that way we won't have to ruin a perfectly good airplane.'

"There's such a thing as too cautious," Bill added. "So if it can be done safely, do it. This is Alaska, and airplanes are the way people travel. But it's the pilot's job to keep it safe. A good pilot can handle one problem, maybe two, but watch out when it keeps stacking up. If you overload the airplane—and overloading is so common many pilots don't even realize they're doing it—then maybe the carburetor heat sticks on, or a few spark plugs give out, and then you get in a downdraft, you're in trouble."

From her kitchen, Barbara said, "Even though you've spent a fortune for insurance, you never want to use it."

"That's the bookkeeper talking," Bill said with affection. "If you need an engine part that few women in the world should understand, Barbara will have it ordered and en route by way of the only outfit in the country that won't ship it through Chattanooga, Tennessee, first."

The afternoon was fading. Bill shook my hand and said, "You better go now. You don't have much light." Mike drove us to Beluga Lake. "Thanks for coming down," he said. "I've always wanted to hear Bill open up like that."

We roared down the lake, climbed skyward, and headed north over the forested, snow-swept Kenai Peninsula. Over the looking glass. The lights of Anchorage twinkled at dusk as we landed with ten minutes to spare.

That night my phone rang. "Hello, Kim. This is Bill. I just want to remind you there's lots of good bush pilots and air taxis in Alaska that have excellent safety records and good working relationships in their communities. This is nothing unique down here. I'm just an ordinary guy doing my job and enjoying it."

Melanie called from the other room, "Who was that?"

"Oh, just an ordinary guy."

Overleaf: Wings of Alaska's Cessna 206 flies above Douglas Island with Juneau between the Coast Range and the Gastineau Channel.

■ *Left:* Temsco Airlines' Cessna 185 pilot Nick Merfeld delivers mail at Nichin Cove. ■ *Above:* Park Ranger Hollis Twitchell loads Lake Clark National Park's Super Cub with cans discarded along the Mulchatna Wild and Scenic River. The bush pilot rule is: Pack it in; pack it out. ■ *Overleaf:* Chris Soloy maneuvers a Hughes 500 helicopter to capture a cow caribou. Biologists of the Alaska Department of Fish and Game and the National Park Service will radio-collar her.

■ *Above:* Fishing stories are shared on the dock as a Beaver taxis toward an Otter tied up by Silver Tip Lodge at Judd Lake. ■ *Right:* West of Knik Arm of Cook Inlet, private pilot Robert Newell enjoys a crystal-clear winter afternoon of flying in his Cessna 180 equipped with wheel-skis. ■ *Following page:* A Wings of Alaska Cessna 206 appears tiny and insignificant flying past the breathtaking granite spires that rise from the Juneau Icefield along the coast of Southeast Alaska.

■ *Left:* A Cessna 180 from Alaska Island Air flies above icebergs calved from the LeConte Glacier. Outgoing tides float bergs from LeConte Bay into Frederick Sound. Avoiding icebergs during takeoffs and landings are of utmost importance to Southeast Alaska float plane operators. ■ *Above:* ERA Helicopters' Bell 206-B Jet Ranger flies past the cruise ship *Fairsea*. Both are heading up Resurrection Bay to a rendevous in Seward where cruise passengers may elect to go flightseeing.

Homeward bound, Mike Meekin flies his Super Cub over the Chugach Mountains to his backyard airstrip.

■ *Above:* A Super Cub's tundra tires provide sufficient surface area to ride on top of packed snow during takeoff from the fifteen hundred-foot Bonanza Hills airstrip. Deeper and softer snow calls for pilots to trade wheels for skis. ■ *Right:* Alaska Coastal Airlines' Beech 18 flies over the slopes of Douglas Island south of Juneau. Built in 1942, this Twin Beech flew in the U. S. Air Force, then sat in a field near Roseburg, Oregon, for twenty years before a trip to Alaska for restoration.

■ *Left:* Retired manager of Iliamna Flight Service Station, Howard Bowman pumps water from the float compartments of his Stinson Voyager 108 during his preflight maintenance at Lake Clark's Hardenburg Bay. ■ *Above:* A Piper Pacer taxis across fog-shrouded Hardenburg Bay. The pilot decides that safety dictates waiting for the fog to dissipate before takeoff. September mornings often bring dense fog when cool nighttime air settles over the relatively warmer lake water.

Leon Alsworth's 1946 Taylorcraft BC-12-D gently banks over Chulitna Bay of Lake Clark. Based on a pre-World War II design first manufactured in 1938, Taylorcrafts remain popular bush planes across the north. In pilot vernacular, "T-Crafts," "T-Crates," and "T-Carts" are assorted nicknames for this two-seater aircraft.

Chapter Five

THE HAINES BIG MAC ATTACK

by Kim Heacox

Haines Airways' Piper Cherokee 180 takes a flight-seeing tour near Glacier Bay National Park's Muir Inlet.

Haines, Alaska, is a nice town. Folks there say they have everything they need. That is why they live there. They build their homes, raise their families, and make a living doing whatever they can. They meet at the Fogcutter Bar to shoot pool, drink beer, and talk about the next salmon, herring, or halibut opening. On clear days, the surrounding Chilkat Mountains are spectacular. And on rainy days, folks slip on a sou'wester and rubber boots, and perhaps join friends at the local bakery for conversation and morning coffee, black with a little sugar.

Then one day in the fall of 1987, a fisherman walked into Haines Airways, the smallest air taxi in town, and chartered a round-trip flight to Juneau, sixty-six nautical miles to the southeast down Lynn Canal. "It cost him 225 bucks," says Mike Shallcross, Chief Executive Officer at Haines Airways. "He wanted to go immediately, so we took him."

Compared to Haines, Juneau is a city. The capital of Alaska, Juneau has traffic jams, high-rise buildings, bureaucracies, and fifteen times the number of people—all things Haines neither wants nor needs. That is, until McDonalds came to Juneau. The fisherman flew down, walked into the epitome of all fast-food restaurants, ate two Big Macs, and then flew back to Haines grinning like a Cheshire cat. People could not stand it. Suddenly everyone in Haines wanted a Big Mac.

The mission was obvious. The Haines Quick Shop, a new convenience store looking for a way to promote their grand opening, decided with Haines Airways—a small, locally-owned operation—that rather than take the people to the burgers, they would bring the burgers to the people. Soon, advertisements peppered the newspapers and radio, and hundreds of orders began to flow in. The great day arrived, and Ken Tyler, Mike's stepson from New Zealand, took off for Juneau piloting a Piper Cherokee Six. Haines waited; the weather worsened.

After farming in Canada for a few years, Mike Shallcross had journeyed to New Zealand to earn a pilot's license. He returned to North America with that and more—namely Barbara, his flight instructor and the woman he would

marry. Barbara's son, Ken, also a pilot, came with them. They settled in Georgia for a while, before moving to Alaska. "All we really wanted to do up here was retire," says Mike. "You know—look at sunsets, fly to Kodiak, go fishing, that kind of thing. Now look at us. We're working fourteen and sixteen hours a day, flying people over some of the most breathtaking country in the world, and loving every minute of it."

In her soft Kiwi accent Barbara reflects back, "If yer stranded in Georgia and need some help, there's no one to call; but if yer stranded in Alaska. . . . Aye, it's fantastic, 'cause forty people will come ta help ya."

Ken made it to Juneau and loaded five large boxes into the Cherokee, each filled with sixty steaming hot Big Macs. The wind gusted out of the south, the sky darkened, and it started to rain.

Ken phoned Mike: "The weather, she doesn't look good down here."

Mike: "Can you make it?"

Ken: "I dunno. I'll give 'er a try and follow the shore."

Mike: "Do what ya can, Ken. We need those burgers up here, otherwise Haines Airways is gonna look bad."

The pressure was on. The good citizens of Haines had collected at the Quick Shop forming a line from the front counter around every aisle, out the door, and halfway to the post office. First in line was a little old gray-haired lady asking, "Where's the beef?" No burgers would mean insurrection. Revolution. A riot. The end of Haines Airways. Ken taxied down the runway and ascended the stormy skies of Juneau while the people of Haines waited for two all-beef patties with special sauce, lettuce, cheese, pickles, and onions—all on a sesame seed bun.

Ken made his first report from Benjamin Island, just north of Juneau. Five minutes later came his second report from Saint Marys. Dense fog lay ahead, and he would have to swing around it. "Thinking back on it," Mike apologizes, "I shouldn't have pressured Ken like I did. Dispatchers are not allowed to push a pilot. That's our policy." Another safety policy at Haines Airways is that pilots are required to

Scott Vaverka uses muscle for power to unload lumber from Frontier Flying Service's DC-3 at Bettles Field.

radio in to dispatch every five minutes to give their location and status. Five minutes ahead of Saint Marys would be Point Sherman. At all times, Ken should be able to see either the navigation point ahead, or the one behind. If he lost them both (while flying VFR—Visual Flight Rules) he would be in trouble.

Concerned, Mike and Barbara waited for his next call. The fog was patchy, the ceiling low, the wind strong. Because the surrounding mountains were full of magnetite, Ken's compass was useless. But he did have two fishermen on board who could help read the whitecaps below and estimate wind speed and direction. Finally, Ken transmitted from Point Sherman.

"How's your visibility?" Mike asked anxiously.

Ken: "Could be better, but I can see Glacier Point." It was good news, for after Glacier Point was Pyramid Island, and after that the homestretch into Haines.

Emergencies are a fact of life in Bush Alaska. Pilots handle them all the time. Granted, the Haines Big Mac Attack was not an emergency, and Haines—one of only two southeast Alaska communities connected year-round to the outside world by a major highway—is not exactly Bush Alaska. But so what? To see the expressions of those people in line at the Quick Shop, you might have thought they were earthquake victims waiting for rations.

Planes are a true lifeline in Bush Alaska. The FAA says, "Aviation is the only means of year-round transportation for approximately 70 percent of Alaska's communities." Entire villages gather in winter to greet the weekly mail/supply plane. Many children in Bush Alaska grow up enamored with planes, not cars. They get to know the pilots. They learn the makes and models of planes, the engine capacities, the top speeds. Some learn to fly before having a formal lesson, or a sixteenth birthday.

Bush pilots save the lives of many Alaskans, both visitors and residents. When an elderly Athabascan woman suffered a respiratory attack in Stevens Village, on the Yukon River, a pilot who was en route from Arctic Village stopped, picked her up, and delivered her to a waiting ambulance in Fairbanks. When two mariners capsized and swam ashore near Izembek Lagoon, a pilot spotted them, landed, treated them for hypothermia, and flew them to safety. When a logger broke his back near Kake on Kupreanof Island, a pilot delayed his flight from Sitka to Petersburg, picked up the logger, and flew him to Juneau. And when a pregnant woman began to have complications in Chevak, a bush pilot rushed her to Bethel where a medical team waited on the runway. No sooner did he land than she delivered a healthy, six-pound baby boy—in the plane. It happens every year around the state: bush pilots giving an extra measure to help their fellow Alaskans.

When the Cherokee Six roared through the skies over Haines on that stormy September day, hope sprang eternal. Mike was at the airport to meet Ken when he landed. The fishermen helped load the Big Macs into a van and then asked to ride with the burgers to the Quick Shop. "Haines Airways always delivers passengers before freight," Mike says, "But these guys were having so much fun they didn't want to miss anything." Perhaps, too, they were hoping for a Big Mac.

No such luck, "I'll take ten," said the old lady at the front of the line. The second customer took six. The third also took six. . . . And so on until the Big Macs were gone. "There were lots of disappointed people," says Barbara, referring to those at the end of the line with still-growling stomachs, "so we flew back down to Juneau the next day and brought back another load." Everything went smoothly. The Big Mac attack ended, and Haines Airways upheld their reputation for reliability. "People are still surprised when I climb into the cockpit," says Barbara. "They're not accustomed to a woman pilot."

"Barbara is a superb pilot and flight instructor, but she's soft spoken and gracious and doesn't flaunt her abilities," says Mike, who is obviously proud of his wife. Barbara smiles. Then he laughs and recalls an incident when she stepped out of character. "Yes," Barbara admits sheepishly, "My plane was loaded with passengers and baggage, and I had climbed into the cockpit when suddenly this fisherman

Natalie Bay of McCarthy Air traded Australia's outback for Alaska's bush.

in the back said, 'Hey, wait a minute, are you the pilot? Isn't there somebody else? I don't need some *woman* pilot.' He had probably assumed I was the baggage handler. I turned to him and said, 'That's right, I'm the pilot. So either get off this plane right now, or fasten your seat belt and shut up.'" He stayed.

If women pilots seem rare in Alaska, look again. They fly every corner of the state. Take Natalie Bay. Born, raised, and schooled in Brisbane, Australia, she became a cartographer with the Australian government and went to New Guinea where she learned to skydive. She jumped in world competition as a member of the Australian team, but soon realized that despite all the fun there was not much future in skydiving. One thing led to another, and she eventually earned her pilot's license. After a couple thousand hours flying the Australian Outback, she came to Alaska to join a friend who was "flying salmon off the beaches" of Bristol Bay. Little did she realize that once the wild magic of Alaska grabbed hold of her, it would not let go. But it was Alaska, and it was worth it.

Today she lives in McCarthy with her husband, Kelly, a former rodeo rider and dog musher, and now a pilot who, like Natalie, loves the solitude of the Wrangell Mountains. Together with their friends, Gary and Nancy Green, they operate McCarthy Air and spend summers flying people around Wrangell-Saint Elias National Park and Preserve, the largest national park in the United States—nearly six times the size of Yellowstone. Kelly and Natalie still manage to get back to Bristol Bay, usually in the fall, but winter finds them home in McCarthy. Last January, Kelly was out repairing his damaged Super Cub. "Yeah," he says, "the tail was all busted up and surrounded by moose tracks. Near as I could tell a young bull thought the plane's tail was an opponent, so he worked it over with his antlers."

Then there is Ellen Paneok, twenty-nine, half Eskimo, quarter Cherokee, and quarter German/Irish. "Yep, that's me," she says in her syncopated, melodic voice. "I got bit by the bug and started flying when I was sixteen, two years before I learned to drive a car. At first all I wanted to do was aerobatics and crop dusting." Today she flies commercially for Cape Smythe Air in Barrow, the northernmost settlement in Alaska. "People that fly up in Barrow are crazy," she says. "Including me. They're crazy for wanting to fly out in the middle of nowhere in the pitch black darkness, blowing snow, and minus 39 degrees. When I first started flying I never dreamed I'd end up in Barrow, on the Arctic Slope." Born in Kotzebue and raised in the Anchorage-Wasilla area, Ellen flew out of Kotzebue, Bethel, Saint Marys, Aniak and McGrath before zipping north to Barrow for a visit. Being Eskimo, a woman, and a pilot certainly caught people's attention. Barrow Air offered her a job on the spot. Then a year later she switched to Cape Smythe Air, the second air taxi in town and a former trading post and whaling company. "I've got relatives everywhere," she says, laughing. "The president of Cape Smythe is related to me somehow, and so are the people at Barrow Air. Come to think of it, I'm related to people all the way from Nome to Barter Island. Seems like every time I go out to another village I meet relatives I didn't know. I'm lucky to have places to stay in every village on the Slope if I happen to get stuck by the weather.

"There's only two air taxis and about ten pilots out of Barrow, and they fly the whole North Slope. We all listen to one frequency and know everybody's locations and altitudes. We tell jokes on the radio, and we've even gone so far as to sing to each other. It's great fun; I wouldn't fly up here if it wasn't."

As Ellen talks she seems to drift away into the Arctic skies, dressed in parka, hood, mittens, and vapor barrier boots, her voice reflective, her eyes on her automatic direction finder, altimeter, and a half dozen other instruments of a Cessna 185 or 207. She follows the coast, for to venture out over the Arctic Ocean in a single engine plane requires more of a gambler than Ellen Paneok. She talks about when she saw the sun break the horizon in late January after not having seen it for two months; when she saw thirty-five polar bears along one five-mile stretch of coast; when she flew television crews out to film two gray whales trapped in

Butch Williams taxis his Cessna 180 on Wrangell Narrows at Petersburg.

the ice, and the Russian icebreakers and Eskimos with chainsaws working to free them; and when she was flying on instruments five hundred feet over ground fog and blowing snow, and suddenly saw hundreds of migrating caribou. "They looked like they were floating. I couldn't see the ground or the sky, and there was absolutely no horizon. It was a total whiteout. But just below and all around me were caribou, floating on the fog."

The Arctic has its mirages and magical displays of perihelions, sun dogs, aurora borealis, and ice fog—all of it strangely beautiful, and none of it new to Ellen. But the beauty has its dangers. The weather takes no prisoners. As sailors of yore said of seas unknown: "Beyond this place there be dragons." Check your plane, watch your instruments, stay alert.

Recently, on a mail run from Atqasuk to Barrow, Ellen was alone in the Cessna 185 when her face started to go numb. At first, she thought it was just the cold air. Then her hands went numb, and her feet and legs. Pretty soon, she found it hard to breathe. "I started to get scared," she says, "but I didn't know what the problem was." Her eyes began to swell, and she could barely see Barrow two miles ahead. She managed to land and get the plane on the ramp, but when she stepped out, she collapsed and hit her head on the ski. Friends picked her up and helped her inside, where she collapsed again. They rushed her to the hospital where she was diagnosed with carbon monoxide poisoning. "I was lucky," she says. "The doctor told me that if I'd been in the air a couple more minutes I would have passed out while flying."

The problem was a faulty engine part that leaked exhaust into the cockpit. During her recovery, Ellen took a break to visit family in Wasilla. It was early December and she had already flown thirteen hundred hours that year. "It gave me a chance to work on my antique airplanes," she says, "I've got four of them (in Wasilla). One is a 1933 Stinson SRJR. Only about five or six were ever made. This particular one has been in Alaska since 1940. The Flying Finn flew it for awhile, so did Archie Ferguson."

When she is not in the air flying, Ellen carves ivory. "That's what supports me—the ivory. Flying supports my antique planes. You know, my father works for the FAA in San Diego and wonders sometimes what I'm doing up here flying around the Arctic and collecting old planes. I suppose I'll always be a renegade, but I want him to be proud of me. It's important."

Flying can reach deep into your heart and marrow. You need not be a pilot—just as you need not be a bird—to be touched by flying. Just immerse yourself in the whole idea. Think of Kay J. Kennedy, now eighty-four, a former award-winning Alaskan reporter, who twenty years ago decided to embark on the biggest writing project of her life: a comprehensive book on the history of Alaska civil aviation. She sold the land on which she had planned to retire, spent two small inheritances, drained all her savings, and exhausted two Volkswagen buses driving to interview more than 300 persons involved in Alaska aviation, including over 150 pilots. If piled in a stack today, her files would reach twenty-five feet high. But after six operations for glaucoma and cataracts, Kay J. Kennedy's eyesight is poor. She will never write her book. "I have run out of money and time, and now I'm running out of eyesight," she once said from her apartment in Fairbanks. "You know, nobody lives forever."

Back in Haines, Barbara Shallcross thinks about those special moments in the skies of Alaska. "I remember one woman last summer," she says. "I took her flightseeing over Glacier Bay on a spectacular evening. She didn't say much; she just looked out the window. But after we landed she asked me to step around the plane so we could be alone. 'I'm dying of cancer,' she told me. 'I was feeling pretty sorry for myself, but when I watched you fly that plane and I saw the majesty of that bay with those beautiful mountains and glaciers, oh my, I realized how small my problems are in the whole scheme of God's great things. Thank you for that flight, Barbara. I'll never forget it.'"

Right: Tony Wilson repairs a Pratt and Whitney R-2800 CB16 engine for Everts Air Fuel's DC-6. The company restores DC-6s and C-46s.

■ *Left:* With flaps down, a Piper Super Cub settles toward a landing in the Bonanza Hills. Assigned to the National Park Service, the Cub is shuttling fuel for caribou research. ■ *Above:* A Cessna 180 on floats practically disappears against glacially carved spires near the Devils Thumb on the Alaska-British Columbia border northwest of Petersburg. ■ *Overleaf:* Arctic light at 10 p.m. casts a magical glow beyond a Cessna 185 float plane on Iniakuk Lake in the Brooks Range.

■ *Above:* Wright Air's Helio Courier H-295 flies near the Wood River south of Fairbanks. Designed by faculty members of Harvard and Massachusetts Institute of Technology, the Helio Courier has incredibly short take-off and landing capabilities. ■ *Right:* At Glacier Creek in Wrangell-St. Elias National Park, McCarthy Air's Kelly Bay drops off hikers from Israel and picks up American backpackers. The Goat Trail through the nearby Chitistone Gorge is spectacular and rugged.

■ *Left:* West of Iliamna Lake, Lake Clark Air Service's Otter places a party of hunters on one of the thousands of unnamed lakes in Alaska. ■ *Above:* Ed Gillet wades from a Wings of Alaska Cessna 206 through the glacial silt to the shore of Muir Inlet. He is carrying gear for a kayak trip in Glacier Bay National Park.

Glaciologists from the Alaska Geophysical Institute protect gear from the rotor wash of Kenai Air Alaska's Bell 205 helicopter departing Redoubt Volcano's 8,400-foot summit crater. Nearly one hundred feet of ice cores drilled by the research team sampled less than three years' precipitation. The scientists determined that, if melted, more than twenty feet of liquid falls annually. Interestingly, most of the precipitation feeding the Drift Glacier comes as summer snow.

Spawned by the heavy snowfall over the Harding Icefield, Bear Glacier flows down to tidewater in Kenai Fjords National Park. Flightseeing passengers on board ERA's Bell 206-L Long Ranger receive an eagle-eye view of the dark bands of rubble, called medial moraines, that run down the length of Bear Glacier.

Pilot Mike Mills jumps off the float of his Beaver as it coasts to the shore of Neka Bay on Chichagof Island. Evidence of much practice, Mike expertly times his leap so he does not fill his hip boots with water, but still has enough water depth to stop the plane's forward motion before the floats grind into the rocks along the shore.

Balloon tires, ideal for the beaches of Bristol Bay, hang below a modified L9B Stinson departing from Naknek.

The shadow of a Cessna 206 races across the tundra past hundreds of caribou of the Northern Alaska Peninsula Herd. Mount Martin, the volcano on the horizon, is within Katmai National Park. This caribou herd seasonally wanders across thousands of square miles of open country between Katmai and Port Moller.

A load of fire extinguishers is removed from a Casa C-212 Aviocar, built in Spain for short, rough airstrips.

■ *Above:* A Super Cub looks like a toy when taxiing beyond a Frontier Flying Service DC-3 at Bettles Field. ■ *Right:* A Beaver taxis across the surface of the Juneau International Airport float pond. Glassy water holds floats on the surface for a longer period of time than choppy water. ■ *Following Page:* Once on step, a Cessna 185 quickly gains the speed necessary for takeoff from a shallow lake west of the Alaska Range near Telaquana Lake in Lake Clark National Preserve.

Taquan Air Service brings a family from Metlakatla, Southeast Alaska's southernmost village, to Ketchikan.

■ *Left:* From Metlakatla to Barrow and Shemya to Northway, per capita, Alaskans fly three times more than other Americans. At Point Lay, passengers help carry freight from Cape Smythe's Twin Otter. ■ *Above:* The Twin Otter's two turboprop engines provide an extra margin of safety for Arctic Ocean flying. Cape Smythe's distinctive polar bear logo greets passengers from Barter Island to Nome. Live polar bears are frequently seen by passengers during flights over pack ice.

At Camp Shaheen Point in Hasselborg Lake, Ed Keller waves from the cockpit of his Lake LA-4 Buccaneer.

Spray flies from the hull of an amphibious Lake Buccaneer that is taking off from Hasselborg Lake in Admiralty Island National Monument. A distinctive flying boat, the Buccaneer has a single engine mounted on pylons above the cabin. The propeller, in an unconventional pushing position, spins high above the water.

A Cessna 180 from Alaska Island Air flies over salt marsh where Duck Creek drains into Frederick Sound. Over the years, the ebb and flow of the tidewater has eroded an intricate mosaic of serpentine channels. A constantly changing panorama of spectacular scenery unfolds beneath those who fly Alaska's skies.

■ *Above:* The season for ski flying generally lasts from November until April. Long, clear days in late winter are great for ski landings. Here, the afternoon sun illuminates the tail of a Piper Pacer and a nearby Super Cub. ■ *Right:* Secure tie-downs hold an Aeronca Sedan and a Piper Super Cub on Lake Hood's surface.

Afterword

REFLECTIONS

by Jay Hammond

Jay Hammond, a former Governor of Alaska, lands his Cessna 180 in Hardenburg Bay at Port Alsworth.

One afternoon on a gray October day, we were flying far down the Alaska Peninsula, which thrusts like the chin whiskers of a belligerent Uncle Sam westward toward Asia. Ragged banks of fog and snow squalls clogged the valley leading to the mountain pass I hoped to thread. Thirty-knot gusts from the southeast bucked over the ridges and clawed at my Cessna 185 floatplane. The turbulence bounced us like a mouse batted by a cat. My concentration oscillated from a rock-strewn stream bed fifty feet below, to canyon walls just off my wing tips, to the gray curtain ahead.

Suddenly, from just behind me came a drunken moan followed by frantic thrashing. My fingers sought the comfort of the .44 Magnum revolver stashed under my seat. I glanced at my huge passenger. Mouth frothing, he floundered on the cabin floor. Fixed on me were his evil, red-rimmed eyes—discomfiting as twin barrels of a shotgun.

"Please, Lord," I breathed in silent supplication. "Please let those ropes hold."

I winged the Cessna around and headed back downstream. The last thing I wanted was to try placing a bullet between those piglike eyes if my passenger freed himself and attacked. The cabin of a Cessna 185 seems mighty small when a crazed passenger goes berserk. How could I get my aircraft safely out of that troubled sky—and myself unscathed with it? I had agreed to haul my passenger, not kill the both of us.

After he had terrorized a number of people, the authorities had chartered my plane. Although he was sedated, it took several men to truss him in a strait jacket and load him aboard the aircraft.

"You have at least two hours before he recovers," the arresting officers declared. Since my destination was less than two hundred miles away and the floatplane cruised at 125 miles per hour, it appeared I had ample time. But I was unaware of bad weather sneaking into my flight path. After an uneventful hour and a half, fog, snow squalls, and scud

Left: East of Beluga Mountain, with water dripping from its floats, a Turboprop Beaver lifts off one of the many unnamed lakes in Alaska.

had enveloped us, forcing a change in course. And now, my passenger had aroused from his stupor.

While his bonds were strong enough so long as he was tranquilized, I doubted they would hold once he fully recovered, and I did not care to find out. Locating a suitable lake, I landed and taxied toward the beach. Once aground, revolver in hand, I leaped out and slogged around to the passenger door. Though his protests were increasing, I was able to cut some of his lashings. I grabbed his legs and hauled his bulk through the aircraft door. He flopped onto the floats like a sack of potatoes, then rolled into the water.

Reluctantly rejecting an inclination to let him slip beneath the surface, I grabbed a handful of hair, held his head above water, and cut the remaining bindings of his canvas strait jacket. When he recovered enough to keep his head above water, I backed off and waited while he hauled his 600-pound carcass to shore. With tooth-popping coughs, my passenger—an Alaskan brown bear—wobbled up the beach and out of sight into the alders.

During the more than forty years I have flown the Alaska bush, my passenger list has included momentarily expectant mothers (fly low, altitude brings on labor), freshly apprehended murderers, live beluga whales, seals, wolves, wolverine, coyotes, caribou calves, moose, swans, and bears. I have also flown people who had been injured or frostbitten, or those whose bodies had been frozen solid, as well as other unfortunates who had died from heart attacks, drownings, or other terminal events. An assortment of unhappy endings seems to lie in wait for the ill-prepared, unfit, or imprudent who venture into Alaska's remote bush.

Of all my various passengers, few have conducted themselves better than the several tranquilized brown bears I have hauled. One exception involved the redecoration of my aircraft's interior by a young bear suffering from a gastro-intestinal disturbance. It seemed he had recently consumed a cathartic concoction of vegetation used by brown bears to purge their systems after hibernation.

Although I have flown over virtually all of Alaska's bush country since 1946, I am reluctant to call myself a true bush

A brown bear walks past the MarkAir Express's Cessna 208 Caravan at Brooks Camp in Katmai National Park.

pilot. That name really belongs to those helmeted, white-scarfed stalwarts who, prior to World War II, had pioneered air service into those remote areas where no pilots had previously ventured. Flying strictly by the seats of their pants, they braved frightening experiences unknown to many who flew in their wake. Their Bellancas, Travelairs, Sikorskis, Wacos, Stinsons, and Fokkers were patched together in ways that violated all of the known rules of aerodynamics. Yet, like a bumble bee ignorant of the laws of physics that say it cannot fly, they flew. In threading their way across the vastness of Alaska they cross-stitched together remote villages and brought them into contact with the twentieth century.

Navigation aids such as radio beacons were absent. Instruments were sometimes as primitive—and useless—as a string stretched between two windshield braces, serving as an "artificial horizon" to one old-timer. But he said it made his passengers feel better when he told them its purpose while flying in whiteouts. "I.F.R." in those days stood not for "Instrument Flight Rules," as it does today, but for "I Follow Rivers," a system which anyone who flies much in Alaska must learn, despite today's array of navigation aids.

The classic description of manned flight as "hours and hours of boredom interrupted by moments of stark terror" evolved long after the first true bush pilots ventured into the North. Before then, by all accounts, "stark terror" clearly predominated. Engine and structural failures were common. Most flights were far from routine, with no airway charts, no radio beacons, no runway lights. For that matter, there were few runways. Most villages, mining camps, or traplines required pilots to set down on gravel bars, mud-flats, ridge tops, or beaches. A ballpark served as an airstrip for the bustling city of three thousand called Anchorage. In the winter, ski-equipped aircraft offered comparative safety and wide use—frozen waterways for landings were found almost everywhere. Floats, of course, granted similar advantages in the open-water season.

The same primitive conditions that confronted true bush pilot pioneers, the ones who wrote the primers on Alaskan aviation, still prevailed in many areas when I arrived in Alaska. Few villages had air strips. I have made my share of off-field landings, both the scheduled and unscheduled varieties. Some of the unscheduled ones came with the thirteen engine failures I have experienced. However, by 1946 when I arrived in Alaska, bush flying had moved from the Stone Age at least into the Bronze, or more accurately, the Aluminum. Fabric-covered aircraft were being replaced by those of less flammable and more durable metal.

With World War II came rapid changes. Military airstrips were built throughout Alaska, flight charts were printed, and radio beacons and weather stations networked much of the Territory. However, one thing still kept boredom at bay for Alaskan pilots—the ever-changing panorama of some of the most spectacular real estate to be found anywhere. Few flights are dull when made close enough to the ground that one can tell the difference between wolf and wolverine tracks in the snow, or know whether the fish in the stream just fifty feet below are rainbow trout or silver salmon.

Although I have flown more than ten thousand hours in the Alaska bush, perhaps the only claim I can properly make to being a "bush pilot" is that the first aircraft I owned and flew commercially in Alaska was of the bush pilot era—a ragwing (fabric-covered), tail-skidded biplane Loening amphibian built in 1929. "Old Patches," as the extensively repaired amphibian was accurately termed, was a consistent old bawd. She seemingly cruised, climbed, dove, and stalled at eighty miles per hour. With only a two hundred-mile range, one had to navigate prudently or carry several extra five-gallon cans of gas which could be hand-pumped directly from the cabin into the wing tanks.

Since the Loening had no dual controls, I had to teach myself to fly it. On my first flight I almost flunked. Aircraft of that era had few fripperies such as hydraulics or vacuum pumps. This one had a mechanical hand pump to raise and lower the landing gear. After making a few fairly respectable wheel landings, I decided it was time to head for water.

Carefully cranking the wheels into full retraction as indicated by a moving red pointer, I lined up for my first water

Jay Hammond loads freight on Howard Bowman's Stinson Voyager with PDX Conversion and modified tail.

landing. On the lakeshore was a crowd, mesmerized, I was sure, by the sight of the antique aircraft that was descending just over their heads. Aware of their eyes, I determined I would impress them by my skillful piloting. My intent was to so gently whisper the Loening onto the water that it would barely break the surface tension. "If only the lads back in Jones Junior High could see me now!" chortled the Walter Mitty within me.

Smooth as satin I settled like a cotton ball on the water. Suddenly there was a horrendous wrenching as the nose of the plane plunged beneath the surface. Water geysered into the cabin. Shattered along with my windshield was my self-esteem as I catapulted upside down and backwards.

I unbuckled my seat belt and flopped headfirst to the cabin roof, by then two feet under water. Momentarily disoriented, I took a few seconds to get my bearings, then worked my way to the rear hatch, which was still above water since the air-filled wings provided flotation. I crawled along the aircraft's belly and clung like a bedraggled duck to the vertical stabilizer.

A power boat arrived and I fastened a rope to the tail skid and signaled the captain to turn the aircraft over onto its belly. Slowly the tail came up as the plane pivoted on its wings. Just a foot or two more and it would have flopped over, upright again. With a dull pop and a shower of spray, the rope broke. Old Patches settled back, then slipped another five feet into the water to rest on the bottom. All that projected from the water was two feet of stabilizer.

The next day we exhumed the Loening from her watery grave, using inflatable life rafts. Investigation showed that the worm gear on the wheel retraction system had slipped. While the indicator showed "wheels up" and could be cranked no farther, the wheels were really only half retracted. This is what prompted that spectacular handspring before my astonished audience.

A few months later I did an even more sensational encore on a high mountain lake. Mercifully, this time there was no audience. It was the end of hunting season, and I was hauling bear hides and gear one hundred fifty miles to Anchorage. Midway, I encountered heavy fog and was forced to land. When the fog cleared, I prepared for takeoff. Lumbering toward towering spruce trees, I climbed on the step and broke water just in time to clear the trees. Relieved to escape the greenery so close beneath, I eased the stick forward and relaxed my straining muscles which, through levitation, had been trying to aid in liftoff. However, my relief was only momentary. As I roared over the lakeshore ten feet above the trees, there was a sharp explosion. Black engine oil shrouded the windshild, followed by nerve-numbing silence. Believe me, there is no silence quite like that experienced in the wake of engine failure. Certainly nothing on earth can better prompt epithets, panic, or supplication. I employed all three as I plunged blindly from the sky toward the clawing green trees below. The right wings slammed into a tree first and took leave. While still airborne, we cartwheeled around and sheared off the left wings on the ground. The denuded hull tore into some alders, torpedoed through swamp water, and shuddered to a halt perched forlornly atop a beaver dam.

Uninjured save for bruised pride and bank account (my entire wartime savings were invested in the Loening) I salvaged rifle, ax, and some emergency gear, and started the twenty-mile trek back to my home lodge.

Some twenty years later Old Patches was hauled out by helicopter. Looking like a petulant pterodactyl among a covey of less archaic aircraft, it now perches at the Alaska Transportation Museum at Palmer.

In the almost twenty thousand hours I have flown since my first ride in a Monocoupe in 1939, I have had my share of heart-hammering "adventures." However, if you show me an adventure, almost invariably I will show you a stupid mistake. While each of the thirteen aircraft engine failures I have experienced remains vividly etched on my mind, much of my culpability has mercifully blurred with the passage of time.

Although I have not injured myself seriously, I have made a few landings in which I take little pride. One late afternoon, a wan sun bounced spongily atop the mirage of

As heavy fog enshrouds Lake Clark, a Cessna 206 lands in bright sunlight on the channel of Hardenburg Bay.

mountains well out of vision to the west. The thermometer taped to the wing strut read minus 22 degrees Fahrenheit. Below, the snow cover on Ugashik Lake stretched for miles, unblemished save for a set of airplane ski tracks near the shoreline. I circled twice to check for overflow—water on top of the ice. If water is present, the tracks show darker than the surrounding snow. I saw no sign of this hazard, which has broken many a plane and bruised many a pilot.

Although sometimes Ugashik freezes late, and sometimes not at all, I was not too concerned; the ice looked solid. Furthermore, for three days, it had stayed more than 20 degrees below zero. With no wind, we settled into the old ski tracks and taxied toward the beach. Suddenly, with a wrenching crunch, our right ski dropped through the ice, tilting the Piper PA-14 up on one wing.

"Get out," I shouted to Chuck, my passenger. But he was already struggling with the single door in the cabin, which was on his side. Forgetting to unhook his seat belt, his efforts were futile at first.

Then with a second crunch, the left ski went through the ice. We were now sitting waist-deep in searing-cold water. Chuck finally flipped his seat belt loose and floundered out the door. Ice cakes blocked his way. He dived beneath, coming up in front of the right wing. I came up behind it, floundering and gasping from the cold. Our winter flight suits of goose down began to encase us in armor plate as they froze.

As the wings settled level with the ice, we crawled on the left wing toward the beach. Testing the ice, we made our way carefully toward shore, lumbering awkwardly toward a cabin two hundred yards distant—hair frozen into helmets, extremities bone-white with frostbite.

The cabin was unlocked. We checked the small oil stove. No oil. No matches, either. Our immersed aircraft contained sleeping bags, food, and matches, but they might as well not have existed. I cracked out of my flight pants and fumbled in an inner pocket with gray sticks that used to be my fingers. I forked out my metal, waterproof matchcase and managed to open it. Shredding old magazines and

newspapers, we started a fire in the stove's oil pot and fed it twigs of alder—the one wood in Alaska which burns fairly well green. Pain scorched our extremities as we started to thaw. We slumped naked on boxes that served as seats, glanced at one another, and started to laugh like idiots, surprised to find we were still alive.

For two days, we fed the fire, remaining unfed ourselves. The cabin had no food; though caribou roamed nearby, we had no way of killing. Chuck, an avid smoker, found some stale coffee and, in an attempt to stave off nicotine withdrawal pangs, rolled coffee grounds in magazine paper and attempted to smoke it, almost asphixiating us both.

On the first day, patches of ice fog rolled in. We heard an aircraft fly over high, but could not see it. However, early the following morning, the sky was clear, and a search plane landed on a small nearby lake to pick us up.

Recently, I flew the hour and a half into Anchorage from Lake Clark with my neighbor and friend, Glen Alsworth, who owns Lake Clark Air, a small air taxi firm. Glen demonstrated his new Loran navigational aid, making a precision flight that ended in an after-dark silk-smooth landing. I was especially impressed since I have not flown instruments since the days I taught instrument flying.

Glen is one of that rare breed who seems to *wear* his airplane—not just climb into it—integrating flesh, bone, and brain with the plane. I have no doubt but that he could have matched exploits with the most venturesome of old-time bush pilots had he been born some fifty years earlier.

Glen's father, Babe, came north in the 1930s, helping pioneer bush flying in the fish-rich Bristol Bay area. Ever since the late 1800s, cannery workers and fishermen have flooded into the Bay in the summers, following the largest runs of red salmon in the world. Float-equipped aircraft proved the best way to transport people and equipment to and from canneries previously accessible only by boat.

Glen remains at the family home on Lake Clark, one hundred eighty roadless miles southwest of Anchorage. His Lake Clark Air operates six aircraft and employs four pilots, providing indispensable services to the area's year-around

Fourth-generation Alaskan bush pilot Trapper Alsworth prepares to take off.

residents. Recently, Glen purchased a helicopter, primarily for emergency flights, since foul weather and ice break-up may keep fixed-wing aircraft grounded.

The winter months reduce Glen's air fleet to serving local residents, transporting between the few nearby Indian and Eskimo villages, hauling freight from Anchorage, or emergency flights. But with the long daylight hours of spring, activity accelerates. Between May and October Glen's aircraft fly almost continuously. Some days, he makes three or more round trips to Anchorage hauling sport fishermen, hunters, prospectors, sightseers, or freight into a region best known for its sport fishing and hunting. With no overland or water access into Lake Clark, its small population is totally dependent on aircraft for fuel, groceries, building materials, and transportation.

Babe taught all of his children to fly and at seventy-eight still holds his pilot's license. For some reason, Glen was a little later learning to fly than his brothers: they soloed at age twelve. Glen waited until he was all of fourteen. Now flying for Glen is his nephew, Leon, representing the third generation of Alsworths to fly the bush commercially.

On Sunday mornings, Glen takes time off from flying to conduct church services for the half-dozen local families which make up the entire population of Port Alsworth. An ordained minister, Glen takes quite literally the biblical admonition to make a joyful noise unto the Lord.

Like all current air taxi operators, Glen holds an instrument rating and is qualified to fly single- and twin-engine aircraft. While major commercial air carriers may have larger, faster, more sophisticated aircraft, pilots like Glen carry on the old bush pilot tradition in an updated fashion while serving as mailmen, ambulance drivers, and transporters in much the same manner as did pilots of old.

While most Alaskans accept flying in small aircraft as the way of life in Alaska, the hazards of such travel greatly exceed that of flying in large planes. Most residents can name friends or family who have perished in small-plane accidents. Glen has lost two members of his immediate family this way. Nonetheless, these are hazards that are are accepted by the majority of Alaskans. We do not dwell on them unduly.

Most problems and fatalities among the flying fraternity I have known have been caused by someone's trying to buck bad weather. Unfortunately, too often bad weather bucks back. Pilots who carry with them adequate emergency equipment and mentally prepare themselves to land and wait out bad weather have a much greater survival rate.

I was fortunate to arrive in Alaska during a time of transition from the virtually roadless frontier to the modern, if still semi-roadless, state it is today. Still flying when I arrived were some of the true old-time bush pilots who blazed many aerial trails. Many I was privileged to know personally: Sig and Noel Wien, Bob Reeve, Ray Peterson, Mud-hole Smith, Sam White, and Archie Ferguson are a few. Their names now may be legend, but their exploits require no fabrication. Like most true pioneers they flashed but briefly across the horizon of history. By opening up the country to those who came in their wake, they wrote a chapter in the saga of the developing transportation system of Alaska which few modern pilots could or would even want to plagiarize.

When I arrived in Alaska, there were seventy-two thousand inhabitants in an area a fifth the size of continental United States. Since I thought Alaska a bit crowded then, you will understand why I now find the state teeming with a population of over five hundred thousand. Nonetheless, in Alaska there remains sufficient room in which even an old crowd-shunning bushrat like myself can still stretch both spirit and imagination.

While many doors are now closed on the freedoms and opportunities prevailing here in the early days, Alaska has not yet been transformed to the "Manhattan on the Muskeg" to which some have aspired. Its star-sweeping mountains, unfathomed lakes, thundering rivers, and long-silent valleys remain largely unchanged from the days when airborne pioneers first viewed them. To follow the flight paths they charted is to link oneself to a colorful past, enriching one's life forever.

■ *Left:* Open, sandy beaches along the Arctic Ocean invite exploration. Pilot Glenn Hittson inspects a century-old wreck of a whaling ship at Point Franklin. ■ *Above:* Glenn flies Cape Smythe Air's owner, Tom Brower, in a Super Cub over myriad ponds and lakes along the Arctic Coastal Plain east of Barrow. ■ *Overleaf:* A brilliant rainbow arcs over the Southeast Alaska community of Petersburg as Alaska Island Air's Beaver flies above Wrangell Narrows toward the Coast Range.

■ *Above:* Horse, Colt, Shelter, and Lincoln islands spread below Wings of Alaska's Cessna 206 heading toward Admiralty Island. Over a thousand islands along the length of the panhandle make Southeast Alaska a dream world for seaplane pilots. ■ *Right:* Wings with massive slotted flaps on leading and trailing edges give the Helio Courier an incredibly slow stall speed of thirty miles per hour. Bob Bursiel lifts his Helio Courier from a gravel bar on the Wood River.

■ *Left:* Bush Pilots Air Service's Otter passes over braided channels of the Susitna River en route to Anchorage. When production ceased in 1967, de Havilland had built 466 single Otters. More than 50 percent still operate. ■ *Right:* Temsco Helicopters' Aerospatiale AStar 350B cruises above a glacially dammed lake during spring break-up. Today's bush pilot may be at the controls of a sophisticated helicopter or in one of the fixed-wing aircraft that opened our last frontier.

ACKNOWLEDGMENTS

This book was made possible by the tremendous support and enthusiasm of the aviation community in Alaska. We acknowledge flying services and organizations, pilots and other people who, in the Alaskan style of pulling together, got the job done. We owe them our deepest gratitude.

In traveling to all corners of our largest state, we shot more than twelve thousand frames for the 192 photographs in the book. A dozen volumes could have been filled with the fun, fascinating, and occasionally white-knuckle tales told.

We only wish the limitations of space, time, and difficult Alaskan weather could have vanished to include all the aviators who fly over remote and rugged bush Alaska. To anyone who may have been inadvertently overlooked in these acknowledgments, we extend our deepest apologies.

AIR TAXI SERVICES:

40-Mile Air, LTD
  Tok, AK 99780
Airlift Alaska
  2301 Merrill Field Drive
  Anchorage, AK 99501
Alaska Airlines
  4750 West International Airport Road
  Anchorage, AK 99502
Alaska Coastal Airlines
  1873 Shell Simmons Drive
  Juneau, AK 99801
Alaska Island Air, Inc.
  P.O. Box 508
  Petersburg, AK 99833
Bellair, Inc.
  Box 371, 475 Kalian
  Sitka, AK 99835
Bettles Lodge Air
  P.O. Box 27
  Bettles, AK 99726
Bran-Air
  P.O. Box 6184
  Anchorage, AK 99502
Brooks Range Aviation
  P.O. Box 10
  Bettles, AK 99726
Bush Pilots Air Service, Inc.
  P.O. Box 190389
  Anchorage, AK 99519

Cape Smythe Air
  P.O. Box 549
  Barrow, AK 99723
Delta Air Service
  Emmonak, AK 99581
Diamond Aviation
  P.O. Box 1440
  Wrangell, AK 99929
ERA Helicopters
  6160 South Airpark Drive
  Anchorage, AK 99502
Everts Air Fuel
  Box 60056
  Fairbanks, AK 99706
Frontier Flying Service
  3820 University Avenue
  Fairbanks, AK 99701
Gulf Air
  Yakatat, AK 99689
Haines Airways
  Box 470
  Haines, AK 99827
Harbor Air
  P.O. Box 269
  Seward, AK 99664
Hudson Air Service
  P.O. Box 82
  Talkeetna, AK 99676
K₂ Aviation
  P.O. Box 545
  Talkeetna, AK 99676

Kachemak Air Service
  P.O. Box 1769
  Homer, AK 99603-1769
Katmai Air Service
  4700 Aircraft Drive
  Anchorage, AK 99502
Ketchikan Air Service
  1600 International Airport
  Ketchikan, AK 99901
Ketchum Air Service, Inc.
  P.O. Box 190588
  Anchorage, AK 99519
King Flying Service
  P.O. Box 26
  Naknek, AK 99633
Kupreanof Flying Service
  P.O. Box 768
  Petersburg, AK 99833
Lake Clark Air
  Port Alsworth, AK 99653
MarkAir
  P.O. Box 196769
  4100 West International Airport Road
  Anchorage, AK 99519
McCarthy Air
  McCarthy, AK 99588
Meekin's Air Service
  SRC Box 8513, Mile 115, Glenn Hwy.
  Palmer, AK 99645
Northern Air Cargo
  3900 West International Airport Road
  Anchorage, AK 99501

Pacific Alaska Airlines
   P.O. Box 60047
   Fairbanks, AK 99706
Peninsula Airways
   4851-A Aircraft Drive
   Anchorage, AK 99502
Reeve Aleutian Airways
   4700 West International Airport Road
   Anchorage, AK 99502
Soloy Helicopters
   P.O. Box 872801
   Wasilla, AK 99687
Sound Adventures
   P.O. Box 190146
   Anchorage, AK 99519
Talkeetna Air Taxi
   P.O. Box 73
   Talkeetna, AK 99676
Taquan Air Service, Inc.
   501 Water
   Ketchikan, AK 99901
Temsco Airlines
   1249 Tongass Avenue
   Ketchikan, AK 99901
Wings of Alaska
   1873 Shell Simmons Drive, Suite 119
   Juneau, AK 99801
Wright Air
   P.O. Box 60142
   Fairbanks, AK 99706

OTHER ORGANIZATIONS:

Alaska Aviation Heritage Museum
   4721 Aircraft Drive
   Anchorage, AK 99502
Alaska Department of Fish and Game
Alaska Marine Highway
   P.O. Box R
   Juneau, AK 99811
Iniakuk Lake Lodge
   P.O. Box 80424
   Fairbanks, AK 99708
Ken-Lab, Inc.
   P.O. Box 128
   Old Lyme, CT 06371
Mamiya America Corporation
   8 Westchester Plaza
   Elmsford, NY 10523
National Park Service
   Alaska Regional Office
   Lake Clark National Park
   Katmai National Park
North Slope Borough Search & Rescue
   P.O. Box 69
   Barrow, AK 99723
Scandia House
   P.O. Box 689
   Petersburg, AK 99833
Tactical Air Command
   Langley Air Force Base, VA 23365

PILOTS AND OTHER PEOPLE:

Shorty Allen
Glen Alsworth
Wayne "B" Alsworth
Leon Alsworth
Jeff Anderson
Brett Archer
Mike Archer
Gary Archer
Steve Bailey
Ray Bane
Bruce Batten
Kelly and Natalie Bay
Gregory E. Beam
Ken Bellows
Layton A. Bennett
Michael Branham
Jimmy Branham
Ted Branstetter
Kris Bredehoff
Price Brower
Tom Brower
Paul Keven Bryant
Bob Bursiel
Chuck Caldwell

Glenn Clark
Don Cook
Ron Costell
Steve Cox
Bruce Dale
Tom Dayton
Mike and Helen Dean
Bill and Barbara de Creeft
Vince Doran, Jr.
Mike Doss
Andy Durrett
Steve Elmore
Bob Engelbrecht
Boyd Evinson
Keith Fiedorowicz
Lee Fink
Dean Fosdick
Bernd and Pat Gaedeke
Don E. Glaser
Andy Greenblatt
James Greiner
Gary Gullickson
John Hajdukovich
Ray Halderman
Karen Hansen
Burt Hanson

Joe Harrell
Sherry Hassel
Clark Hassell
Dave Henley
Jamie E. Hittson
Glenn Hittson
Charley Holt
Andy Hutchinson
Mike Ivers
Bob Jacobsen
Jim Jakubek
Larry Jenkins
Kirk and Leslie Johnson
John F. Jones
Chad Allen Jones
Ed Keller
Kay J. Kennedy
Ketch Ketchum
Craig Ketchum
Dan and Lynda Klaes
Gene Kunz
George H. Lane
Jim LaRowe
David R. Leschak
Larry Lister
Dana Maros

David McDowell
Mike McBride
Mike and Diane Meekin
Nick Merfeld
Mike Mills
Ivy Moore
Brian K. Nelson
Robert Newell
Gary Nickle
Don Nyberg
Jim O'Meara
Jim Okonek
Chris Olivolo
Loren Olsen
Ellen Paneok
Pat Patterson
Len Paur
Jim Pepper
Sonny Peterson
Ray Peterson
Ludwig Pfleger
John Pletcher
John Reed
Richard Reeve
Janice Reeve
Bob Reinaker

Mike Reynolds
F. Morgan Richardson
Doug Riemer
Dave Riemer
Tyler Robinson
Ed Rogers
Ken and Dawn Rossit
Dane T. Roundtree
Rick Schikora
Damon Schmidt
Jerry and Candy Scudero
Frank Shaffer
Michael and Barbara Shallcross
Mike Sharpe
Rusty Shaub
Roberta Sheldon
Roger Siglin
Craig and Diane Slye
Mike Smith
Doug Solberg
Chris Soloy
Ted Spencer
John Spencer
Dave and Kathy Spokely
Mike Stedman
Bill Stevenson

Richard Stone
Lee Svoboda
Kirk Sweetsir
Rick Swischer
Jerry Taylor
Frank Taylor
Ken Taylor
Lowell Thomas, Jr.
Norman Tibbetts
Hollis Twitchell
Mick Van Hatten
Larry Van Slyke
Jerry Vink
Jimmy Vreeland
Willy Lou Warbelow
Dave Werner
Cliff Westbrook
Alan White
Dave Wilder
Butch Williams
Gordon "Windy" Windell
Wesley Witten
Sam Wright
David Wunsch
Mike Yorke
Douglas G. Young

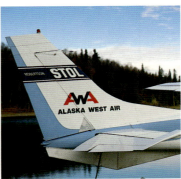